Also by Jan Henson Dow

<u>Nonfiction</u>
Writing the Award-Winning Play (with Shannon Michal Dow.)

<u>Poetry</u>
At the Han-ku Pass

<u>Short Plays</u>
Plays that Pop!: One-Act, Ten-Minute, and Monologues

<u>Full-Length Plays</u>
Dark Passages (with Shannon Michal Dow and Robert Schroeder, published by Popular Play Service.)
Dreamers, Shadows, Dreams (with Robert Schroeder, published by Phosphene Publishing Co.)
The Golden Dawn (with Robert Schroeder, published by Phosphene Publishing Co.)
Killing Dante (with Shannon Michal Dow, published by Samuel French, Inc.)
The Magistry (with Robert Schroeder, published by Popular Play Service.)
The Moorlark (with Shannon Michal Dow, published by Phosphene Publishing Co.)
Shaka (with Robert Schroeder, published by Phosphene Publishing Co.)
That Madcap Moon (with Robert Schroeder, published by Phosphene Publishing Co.)

SHOKO

A Play by

Jan Henson Dow
&
Robert Schroeder

Phosphene Publishing Company
Houston, Texas

Shaka
© 2017 by Jan Henson Dow
ISBN 10: 0-9986316-0-4
ISBN 13: 978-0-9986316-0-8

This play is a work of fiction. Names, characters, places, and incidents either are products of the author's imagination or are used as fiction.

All rights reserved. No part of this work may be copied or otherwise produced or reproduced in any form—printed, electronic, live performance, videotaping, recording, or otherwise—without express permission of Phosphene Publishing Company, except for brief excerpts used in reviews, articles, and critical works.

Published by
Phosphene Publishing Company
Houston, Texas, USA
phosphenepublishing.com

1.1

Cover: A European artist's impression of Shaka with a long throwing assegai and heavy shield (1824).

To
Wendell MacNeal
for directing a great production

Production of *Shaka*

This edition of *Shaka* is dedicated to the reading public only. Professionals and amateurs are hereby warned that the play is subject to production fees. All rights, including professional, amateur, motion pictures, recitation, lecturing, public reading, radio broadcasting, television, and the rights of translation into foreign languages, are strictly reserved.

The amateur live stage performance rights to *Shaka* are controlled exclusively by Phosphene Publishing Company. There is a fee of $35 to produce this play, and the fee must be paid and rights secured in writing from Phosphene Publishing Company at least two weeks prior to the opening performance of the play. The fee must be paid whether the play is presented for charity or by a nonprofit or profit-seeking organization and whether or not admission is charged.

Professional and stock royalty will be quoted on application to Phosphene Publishing Company.

Copying from this book without express permission of the publisher is strictly forbidden by law, and the right of performance is not transferable.

Whenever the play is produced, the following notice must appear on all programs, printing, and advertising for the play: "Produced by special arrangement with Phosphene Publishing Company."

Due authorship credit must be given on all programs, printing, and advertising for the play.

No one shall commit or authorize any act or omission by which the copyright, or the right to copyright, of this play may be impaired.

No one may make any changes to this play in the process of production, or otherwise.

Correspondence and inquiries may be made through the Phosphene Publishing Company website at phosphenepublishing.com.

SHOKO

Cast of Characters
(In order of appearance)

NARRATOR—An ancient African storyteller dressed in a motley and ragged assortment of native and European costume. By putting on different masks and a different costumes, he will take various parts in the play.

THREE LARGE MASKED REED FIGURES—These figures loom over the opening scene, swaying to the sound of the drums.

SHAKA—In the Prologue, Shaka is in his late 20s. He is a magnificent example of manhood, standing 6'3" inches tall. He has a strong, well-proportioned body and is lithe and muscular. He is almost nude. After the prologue, Shaka is about 29 years old. In appearance, he is commanding, born to rule a nation of warriors, with eyes that flash fire and intelligence. He is dressed in a magnificent costume of leopard skins and white fur armbands and leg bands with a headdress centered with a blue crane feather. He carries a white shield with a black spot and a short, stabbing spear, Ixwa, the assegai. He looks every inch a king.

NANDI—Shaka's mother, is in her 40s. She is a woman of dignity, pride, and presence. Throughout the play, she wears a costume that falls from one shoulder but does not expose her breasts.

NOBELA—A witch: Mother of Darkness and of Night. She is shrouded in a cloak that covers her so that it is difficult to see her threatening figure. She is a hag like woman of uncertain age and has an evil face. She is dressed in monkey skins and carries the witchdoctor's fly whisk made of a wildebeest tail.

DINGANE—The eldest legitimate son of Chief Senzangakona. He is half brother to Shaka. He is in his 20s and is of medium height and is heavyset. He is not kingly or particularly brave, but he is an intelligent and a shrewd opportunist.

MHLANGANA—Dingane's brother and half brother to Shaka. Mhlangana is younger than Dingane and of slighter build. Mhlangana is a follower, a man of little courage who obviously defers to his older brother.

MBOPA—The Induna of the dead chief and leaders of the elders of the tribe. He is played by the Narrator.

PAMPATA—A young woman about 24, of regal beauty and presence. Shaka's lover.

PAMPITA'S SERVING WOMAN

MGOBOZI—Shaka's friend, a brave warrior.

YOUNG WARRIOR

MAIDEN

MZILIKAZI—A handsome young warrior.

MAIDEN—Mgobozi's bride.

NANDI'S SERVING WOMAN

TWO MESSENGERS

MALE FIGURE—Wearing the mask of a bull. Filmy red scarves are attached to his body.

TWO MASKED SORCERERS—They are dressed in bizarre costumes and fearsome masks.

CROWD, WARRIORS, WOMEN—Throughout, there are various groups consisting of crowds, warriors, and women representing the people of the Zulu. The warriors bear spears and shields, and some of the figures wear weird and mysterious masks and costumes.

Shaka

ACT I: SCENE ONE (PROLOGUE)

(The stage is in total darkness. It is bare, except for a small campfire DR, which is not yet seen in the darkness. The SOUND of DRUMS has been going on for some time. The whole theatre slowly DARKENS as the SOUND of the DRUMS RISES then FALLS until the DRUMS are BARELY HEARD in the background. There is the mournful SOUND of the WIND RISING. Far to R, a small CAMPFIRE FLARES UP, as if it is the only light in the world. NARRATOR, an ancient African storyteller, crouches by the fire.)

NARRATOR
(NARRATOR warms his hands by the fire and then shivers, holding his tattered cloak more closely about him. Then he looks directly at the audience.)
Listen! Do you hear the sound of the wind? It is the voice of 10,000 spears far away and lost beyond the hills. The spirits are restless tonight and cannot be quiet in their graves. They are all about us, their eyes staring out of the dark. They watch and wait. They wait for Shaka, the Lion!
(HE stirs up the fire.)
Throw more wood on the fire to keep back the spirits of the night, and I will tell you a tale of long ago, when Shaka, the Lion, stalked the land!

(HE rises from the fire.)

Where he walked the earth trembled! When he raised his hands, the rivers ran with blood! At the sound of his voice, men shook and were afraid! Before he lived there were no Zulus, only separate tribes scattered like specks of grain across the plains from the mountains to the sea. After he died, the Zulu were broken and sank back into the earth from whence they came. But we will not speak of that. He is not dead. His spirit walks abroad and will not quit the earth. It cannot find peace while the voice of the living cry to him still. Shaka Zulu!

> OFFSTAGE VOICES
> (Echoing.)

Shaka Zulu! — Shaka Zulu! — Shaka Zulu!

> (SOUND of DRUMS BEAT like a rhythmic heartbeat.)
>
> NARRATOR

In every heart beats the heart of Africa. Do you not hear it? Feel your breast! There the drums speak! Feel your pulse! There the rivers flow!

> (SOUND of BREATHING is HEARD.)

Listen to the sounds in the night of breathing and of drums! That is the voice of Africa calling you home. Listen now to the voice of the drums, and I will tell you a tale of long ago, when Shaka ruled and the sound of his voice shook the world.

> (SOUND of the DRUMS RISE. FLAMES of the CAMPFIRE SINK. Stage is once again in DARKNESS. NARRATOR throws off his ragged costume and puts on animal skins, becoming the BLACKSMITH-SORCERER. Out of the darkness can be seen large African MASKS. SPOTLIGHTS focus on each mask in turn, moving about the stage. STRANGE SOUNDS of WHISTLES, RATTLES, and the WIND, blending with the SOUND of the

DRUMS are HEARD. THREE LARGE MASKED REED FIGURES loom over the scene, swaying to the sound of the drums. At the center Stage Rear, the scene is LIT by a FLAME, which suddenly FLARES UP. NARRATOR/BLACKSMITH-SORCERER, crouching by the fire, works a bellows. SHAKA appears from the surrounding darkness and is silhouetted by the flames.

NARRATOR/BLACKSMITH-SORCERER
Who dares approach the forge of the Nameless One in the dead of night?

SHAKA
Do not threaten me, old man. I am here to hold you to your promise.

NARRATOR/BLACKSMITH-SORCERER
It is you then.

SHAKA
I come for the spear—to be forged as I required.

NARRATOR/BLACKSMITH-SORCERER
Your spear is forged.
(HE makes an imperious gesture and ONE of the masked FIGURES places a short, sturdy spear in the BLACKSMITH'S hands.)
Here it is. The image of your very soul. Brave, sharp, cold, and cruel—implacable as the grave. Child of darkness and of death, from earth and fire it came, and the Nameless One breathed into it the breath of life and it became a living soul.
(SHAKA reaches for the spear.)
Wait! I warn you! Once you take up this spear, you will never let it go. It was forged at the dark of the moon when the signs in the heavens cried of change and a star with a fiery tail flashed across the sky. The liver of a great chief went into the fire. The heart of a brave

warrior and the blood of a newborn babe tempered the blade. If you take this spear, you will master it or it will master you. There is no other way.

SHAKA
(Eagerly grasping the spear.)
Give it to me, old man. I have dreamed of this spear in the night.

NARRATOR/BLACKSMITH-SORCERER
I have warned you!

SHAKA
(Tests the spear in various fighting positions. He thrusts as if stabbing an enemy.)
Ngadla! I have eaten!
(HE raises the spear above his head in triumph.)
Ixwa! *[Pronounced with the glottal click]* This is the spear of my dreams! What is your price?

NARRATOR/BLACKSMITH-SORCERER
What do you possess?

SHAKA
Myself!

NARRATOR/BLACKSMITH-SORCERER
And what is that worth to me?

SHAKA
Whatever you ask. In the eyes of others I am nothing! Shaka, the outcast! Spat upon by my father, the chief! Disowned by my brothers! My mother and I forced to become homeless wanderers! But all of that you know. What is your price?

NARRATOR/BLACKSMITH-SORCERER
Take the spear. It is yours, your very soul. I but send my cattle ahead. When the time comes, you will name the price.

SHAKA
I could pay the price now in your blood, old man. Are you not afraid?

NARRATOR/BLACKSMITH-SORCERER
I have lived a long time and seen many things. I know that look of fire in your eyes. Your word is a spear. Once it is given, you will stand by it for good or ill. Where it goes, you will go.

SHAKA
My word is given. I will pay the price.

NARRATOR/BLACKSMITH-SORCERER
I have no doubt of that. So be it.

(SOUND of DRUMS RISE. BLACKOUT.)

END OF SCENE ONE

ACT I: SCENE TWO

(The same set. The royal kraal of Chief Senzangakona is suggested by a beehive-shaped hut in the background. An open space is in the center of the stage with a fig tree to one side.)

NARRATOR

The old chief, Senzangakona, lies dying in his royal kraal, poisoned secretly by his outcast queen.
(NANDI, Shaka's mother, appears at Stage Left.)
She has enlisted the aid of the witch of the dark path, Nobela, Mother of Darkness and of Night.

(NARRATOR exits as NOBELA appears at Stage Right.)

NANDI

What news? Is the old chief dead?

NOBELA

Patience. These things take time. You asked for a slow dying with much pain and blood.

NANDI

Fool! Not so slowly that Dingane would seize the power. My son must rule or vultures will pick your eyes.

NOBELA

No need to threaten me. I swear your son will rule. I have seen it in the smoke.

NANDI

Go, then, and bring me word when the old chief is dead. If he does not die, you will die in his place.

NOBELA

He will die in agony on a rack of pain. I swear it.

NANDI

Be gone. They must not see you here with me. Send me word when he is dead.

> (NOBELA exits Stage Left. DINGANE appears from Up Right.)

DINGANE

What are you doing here, bitch? My father cast you out. You and your bitch's whelp are not welcome here. I warn you....

NANDI

And I warn you. Who gave you the power to rule? Your father knew you are a liar and your brother a coward and a fool.

DINGANE

You will not talk so bravely when the great chief is dead. Not with your tongue cut out.

NANDI

As long as the chief lives, I am his queen.

DINGANE

Queen? Slut! We shall see what you will be when he is dead.

NANDI

Yes, we shall see what you will be when he is dead.

> (SHE turns and exits Stage Left. MHLANGANA appears from Up Right.)

MHLANGANA

The word we waited for has come. The chief is dead!

DINGANE
Now is the time to act. We are sons by the same mother. Are you with me?

MHLANGANA
Haven't I always covered your back? Do what you will and I am with you.

DINGANE
When I speak, you must acknowledge my right as the eldest son. Then kneel, swearing allegiance to me. The elders will have to follow.

MHLANGANA
What of our father's other sons? What of Shaka? He will never stand still for this.

DINGANE
That bastard upstart! By the time he hears of this, I will have seized the power. The elders will never support him against me.

MHLANGANA
And the others?

DINGANE
If they dare to challenge me, they will eat earth this day. My men are already prepared to execute my orders. First, Shaka must die; then our other brothers one by one.

MHLANGANA
If brothers are to die, then what guarantee do I have, oh brother, that I will live if I risk my life for you?

DINGANE
We have the same mother, you and I, and have suckled the same milk. I will reward you well. Are you with me?

MHLANGANA

Bayete! To the death!

DINGANE

Then all is well. Be prepared. Wait for the signal.

> (HE grabs MHLANGANA'S arm and steps in front of him as MBOPA, the elder of the tribe, played by the Narrator, enters.)

MBOPA

We see you, Dingane, son of the Great Chief, Senzangakona.

DINGANE

We see you, Mbopa, elder of the tribe, wise counselor of the Great Chief.

MBOPA

The Great Chief, your father, has joined his ancestors. The land will be desolate.

DINGANE

The land will be desolate, but a new chief will arise.

MBOPA

Where will he appear?

DINGANE

He stands before you.

MBOPA

That may be. That may be. We, the elders, will decide the matter after proper deliberation. Tradition requires it.

DINGANE

Then decide quickly.

MBOPA
Do you threaten me?

DINGANE
No need to speak of threat. I am his eldest son. Have I not always supported tradition and the council of the elders?

MBOPA
That remains to be seen. The proper ceremonies must be observed.

DINGANE
My brothers are restless. Especially one. He, of a certainty, would not wait for the body to grow cold.

MBOPA
Which brother is this who would defy the spirits and bring ruin upon us all?

DINGANE
Shaka, the despised one, the outcast, born of a casual alliance in the fun of the roads. Shaka has no legitimate claim to my father's house.

MBOPA
Let all these sons appear that they may honor their father with proper mourning.

DINGANE
They do not dare. Like jackals they must wait to smell which way the wind will blow the scent of death.

MBOPA
A chief cannot have the liver of a coward. He must be one fit to lead.

MHLANGANA
(Stepping forward.)
Such a chief stands before you. I bow and swear allegiance to Dingane, King of Kings. Bayete! To the death!

(MHLANGANA kneels before Dingane and puts his forehead on DINGANE'S feet. SOUND of DRUMS RISES. SHAKA suddenly appears at Stage Left with his mother, NANDI. Dressed in a magnificent costume of leopard skins and white fur armbands and leg bands with a headdress centered with a blue crane feather, he looks every inch a king. He carries a white shield with a black spot and his short, stabbing spear, IXWA, the assegai. Two of SHAKA'S WARRIORS appear at Stage Right, spears and shields at ready. SHAKA'S entrance creates concern among ALL those on stage.)

SHAKA
If you wish to join our father in his death, we will mourn you both, oh Dingane.

MBOPA
Who speaks in the presence of the elders?

SHAKA
Shaka, the outcast, and his mother, the queen.

MBOPA
What is this unseemly display with your father drawing his last breath?

SHAKA
I have had word that he has already joined the ancestors.

NANDI
He has already turned green and begins to stink.

DINGANE
Hold your tongue, woman! My father, the Great Chief, spit you out of his mouth like rotten fruit.

SHAKA

Be very careful how you address the mother of the new chief. The old chief was my father, too.

DINGANE

And I am the eldest legitimate son and was named heir while he still lived. You are a bastard. The ancestors are called to witness.

SHAKA

Let the ancestors step forth and witness now. Or perhaps you would go to where they are and ask them yourself.

MBOPA

Would you murder your brother over the body of your own father? It is a time of mourning.

SHAKA

I have come to mourn, and my spear will weep tears of blood.

DINGANE

You will mourn—and your mother with you—when I am chief.

SHAKA

You have said it. When you are chief. You are not fit to rule. Do you think I would leave the people in your hands, surrounded by their enemies, subject to your tender mercies? Not while I live!

DINGANE

I call the elders to witness to my right to rule.

SHAKA

All those who are dead men: Step forth and witness for my brother, Dingane.
> (No one dares to speak. DINGANE starts to make a move and then changes his mind.)

All those who would live: Witness for Shaka Zulu!

ALL
(Except DINGANE, MHLANGANA, and MBOPA.)
Shaka Zulu! Bayete! Shaka Zulu! Bayete! Shaka Zulu! Bayete!

DINGANE
(Moving suddenly.)
You will rule over my dead body!

SHAKA
You have said it.
> (SHAKA gestures, and one of the WARRIORS gives his spear and shield to DINGANE.)

Throw your spear first, but do not miss!
> (DINGANE throws the spear, but SHAKA deflects the spear with his shield.)

Sigidi!
> (SHAKA closes with DINGANE. In a maneuver to become famous as having been originated by him, SHAKA hooks the left side of his shield round the left edge of his opponent's left side. With his short, stabbing spear, SHAKA forces DINGANE to the ground and keeps the spear at his throat.)

Ngadla! I have eaten!

DINGANE
Have mercy! I am your father's son!

SHAKA
Swear allegiance to the new chief of the Zulu!

DINGANE
I swear my allegiance! Live and grow great, oh Chief!

SHAKA
And your brother?

MHLANGANA
I swear! Live and grow great, oh Chief.

NANDI
(To SHAKA.)
Kill them now, my son, or you will live to regret it.

SHAKA
Must I begin by killing my own brothers? You will have power over all the Zulus, Mother, but you will not rule me.
(To DINGANE.)
We had one father, Dingane. Serve me well, and you will live under the protection of my name. Betray me, and I will cut you down like a dry stalk.

DINGANE and MHLANGANA
(Both arise.)
Bayete! Shaka Zulu! Bayete!

ALL
Bayete! Shaka Zulu! Bayete!

SHAKA
Salute the Great Mother of all the people. When she smiles, all will smile. When she frowns, all will tremble before her gaze.

ALL
Bayete! Great Mother! Bayete!

SHAKA
The old Chief has joined his ancestors, and a new chief has risen from the earth.
(To MBOPA.)
Let all the proper ceremonies be observed. Slaughter a black bull and wrap his body in its hide so that all the spirits will know that he was a great chief. Let man and maidservants be killed with proper

ceremony and go beneath the earth to serve him on his long journey to the land of the dead.

MBOPA

It is well that the traditions be observed.

SHAKA

Mark this well, old man, when I speak, I create tradition. If it does not serve me, it will no longer stand. I will tell you what is tradition; you will not tell me. Serve me well and live under the protection of my name.

MBOPA

It is we, the Elders, who hold tradition in our hands and pass it to the young.

SHAKA

Not if your hands are cut off.

MBOPA

Would you overturn the world?

SHAKA

Yes, and create a new one to my liking. With this spear, I will forge a new people, a warrior nation, and the name of Zulu will be like thunder before the coming storm. And the rain of our passing will make the dead land grow rich again. Let the dead past join the ancestors. Which do you choose: to live, or to go with the dead past?

MBOPA

You are, indeed, your father's son, and I am your servant in all things. I live in your shadow, oh Great Chief.

> (HE bows to the ground before SHAKA, touching HIS forehead to the earth.)

SHAKA

You were my father's Induna and will be mine if you serve me well. And my brothers will be councilors while they are loyal to my name.

DINGANE

We live in your shadow and follow you to the death.

(HE and MHLANGANA bow.)

SHAKA

Come, Mother, we have been rootless long enough. I will build a new kraal at Bulawayo and you will rule it in my name.

NANDI

Did I not tell you that you would be great, my Son? I knew it when you suckled at my breast. I knew the fiery look of greatness in your eyes. I dreamed of this moment.

SHAKA

I swear to you. The Zulu will become a great people, and you will be their queen. I will burn the stubble from this land and make a fire to warm your heart. Come, Mother, and choose the place of your great house. Arise, oh Keepers of Tradition. After my father is buried with proper ceremony, burn this kraal to the ground and scatter the ashes to the wind.

(SHAKA and NANDI exit with their WARRIORS. MBOPA exits. DINGANE and MHLANGANA are left in a cleared space. They rise from their knees. DINGANE looks in the direction of Shaka's exit. MHLANGANA starts to speak.)

DINGANE

Be still until I give you leave to speak. Every sun must have its setting and a new one rise. Our time will come.

(As THEY exit, NARRATOR enters. They pass the NARRATOR but are not aware of him because he is telling their story and they exist in an earlier time.)

NARRATOR

Their time will come, indeed. Every sun must have its setting and a new one rise.

(RISING SOUND of DRUMS.)

END OF SCENE TWO

ACT I: SCENE THREE

(RISING SOUND of WAR DRUMS. Leaping FLAMES and shadows of WARRIORS in full battle dress make monstrous shadows against the backdrop.)

NARRATOR

The sound of war drums fills the land.
Like grain the enemy falls; victorious the Zulu rise.
The name of Shaka rolls like thunder before the storm.
The Zulu sing of victory and 10,000 spears.

(SOUND of WAR DRUMS. Off Stage VOICES, chanting.)

WARRIORS

(Entering.)
Stamp our feet! The mountains shake!
Stamp our feet! The mountains shake!
Sigidi! Drink Blood! Nagadla! We have eaten!
Sigidi! Drink Blood! Nagadla! We have eaten!

(A Zulu WARRIOR with spear and shield dances a dance of war and victory. At the climax of the dance, he rushes Offstage, his spear and shield held aloft, followed by the others. NARRATOR exits. At Stage Left PAMPATA appears. SHE is like a young gazelle, poised as if for flight. SHE looks anxiously to Stage Right. Suddenly the DRUMS STOP. SHAKA appears in full battle dress, carrying his shield and spear. He and PAMPATA stand alert and full of tension, very still and looking intently at each other. For a moment, the audience should almost believe that she is a trophy of war, about to be attacked. SHAKA tosses his headdress aside with his spear. With slow grace, he throws his shield flat on the ground between them. She is still poised as if to flee.)

SHAKA
Come, my young gazelle. I want to hold you in my arms.

PAMPATA
My Lion.

(SHE leaps into his arms, and HE catches her, holding her aloft, then slowly lowering her body along the length of his.)

SHAKA
My sleek doe, I want to hear you moan.

(HE slowly lowers HER to the shield and places her on it.)

PAMPATA
My black bull, with the strength of ten.

SHAKA
Wipe the blood from my spear that I may live. Cleanse the ax, for the world is full of death.

PAMPATA
It is born again in my arms.

(The stage is in SHADOWS where they lie. The SOUND of the DRUMS INCREASES. Thrown on the shadows in the background is a dance pantomime of a man and a woman, in a dance of love and longing. As the dance ends, LIGHTS UP SOFTLY on SHAKA and PAMPATA.)

SHAKA
(HE lies on his back on the shield, and SHE leans over him.)
Did the drums speak of our great victory over the Butelezi?

PAMPATA
Yes, the voice of the drums is everywhere, praising your name, Shaka, the bravest of all brave warriors. They say you fought like a madman, and all gave ground before you. I think you fight just as you make love—like one possessed.

SHAKA
Did I possess you, oh my brave battle ground?

PAMPATA
I am weak with your pleasure, my lord. All my defenses are down.

SHAKA
And mine. You are the only warrior strong enough to throw me. You are the other half of my soul, Pampata. See I am at your mercy.
>   (HE throws his arms back in mock surrender.)

I am helpless. Do what you will.

PAMPATA
>   (SHE laughs in playful joy and quickly sits astride his chest, pinning his shoulders to the ground with her hands.)

Ngadla! I have eaten! What ransom would you give to be free?

SHAKA
Who would be free of so sweet a slavery?

PAMPATA
I shall cut out your heart and place it with mine.

SHAKA
Would you retake old ground?

PAMPATA
Yes, again and again!

SHAKA
That was done long ago, when you believed in my name against all odds, even though I was only an outcast with no village to call my own.

PAMPATA
But, oh, what an outcast, a king without a country. Do you remember when you first looked into my eyes?

SHAKA
Yes, and you looked into my eyes, and we were bound with the same cord that makes the bravest king captive after all.

PAMPATA
I would rather hold your heart than rule the strongest land.

SHAKA
And I would rather hold—your sweet ass—but enough of that.
> (With a deft movement, HE flips HER over onto her back, and suddenly they have changed places, with him sitting astride her.)

A king does not rule a warrior nation by lying on his back half the day.
> (HE jumps to his feet and quickly pulls HER upright.)

The taste of victory is short, and my warriors quickly grow restless. He who mounts the leopard has no choice but ride. But first I need a bath, and you will scrub my back.

PAMPATA
Don't I always scrub your back?

SHAKA
If it pleases you.

PAMPATA
It pleases me well. You have but to command, my lord.

SHAKA
I have noticed how quickly you respond to commands. I would sooner command an elephant not to charge.

PAMPATA
Speaking of charging elephants, my lord, your mother is well. She is impatient to see you.

SHAKA
Has she given you a very bad time?

PAMPATA
She will have no rivals for your heart.

SHAKA
She has no rivals, as you have none. Does the hawk sing like the honeybee? This jealousy of women I have no time for. If she presses you too closely, come to me.

PAMPATA
Ha! That would solve everything!
    (Ironically.)
How little men know of women. I will stay out of her way.

SHAKA
Go and prepare my bath, woman. I must see my mother before she sharpens her tongue. But I would have further—word with you.

PAMPATA
And I with you, my lord.

(THEY exit in opposite directions.)

END OF SCENE THREE

ACT I: SCENE FOUR

(A short time after the previous scene. Both the inside and outside of NANDI'S royal hut can be seen. NANDI paces anxiously. A SERVING WOMAN is with her.)

MBOPA
(Entering.)
Great news of victory! The Lion returns victorious, oh Queen.

NANDI
Is he all right? Was he wounded?

MBOPA
He is invincible, oh Queen. No spear could touch him. The people say he has a magic shield that blunts all spears. He will live to celebrate many victories.

NANDI
They are right. My son is invincible! But where is he? Why does he not come to me?

MBOPA
The Great Chief cleanses the ax with Pampata.

NANDI
(With obvious anger.)
Pampata! That bitch! Go, find him. Tell him my heart longs to see him.
    (NOBELA enters. NANDI still speaking to MBOPA.)
Find my son and bring him here to me.

(MBOPA bows and exits.)

NOBELA
(In an eerie, whining voice.)
We see you, Mother of the Great Elephant.

NANDI

We see you, Nobela, Mother of Darkness and of Death. But my son must not see you here.

> (SHE gestures to the SERVING WOMAN, and the SERVING WOMAN exits.)

NOBELA

I have come to congratulate you in our victory.

NANDI

You shall be well paid as always. Your charms have kept my son safe from harm and have brought him home to me.

NOBELA

To you? My spies say otherwise.

NANDI

Hyena's bitch! How dare you

NOBELA

My charms have served you well. They are powerful and dangerous charms. I risked my life for his safety. I wrestled all night with a demon and threw him to the ground. When he entered me, his member was scaly and cold like a great snake.

NANDI

You make me shudder with your words. How can you deal with evil spirits?

NOBELA

To match human deeds, oh Queen. It is we who give them power. They are only smoke until we raise them from the dead.

SERVING WOMAN
(Entering, frightened.)

The Great Chief comes, oh Queen.

NANDI
(To NOBELA.)
Stay hidden. Do not let him see you here.

(NANDI exits from the hut. NOBELA hides within, listening.)

SHAKA
(Enters and strides toward HIS mother.)
Did I see that evil smelling hyena enter your compound? I do not want her near me. She stinks of corpses, and I have had enough of the smell of death for this day.

NANDI
Hush, I have sent her away, but even the walls have ears, and it is not safe to mock one in league with the powers of darkness.

SHAKA
The superstitious rabble fears her power, but I do not. A king makes his own power.

NANDI
Her charms have kept you safe.

SHAKA
As long as she serves my purpose, she will live. But let her threaten me....

NANDI
Let us not quarrel, my son. I have sacrificed to the ancestors for your safe return. Tell me of your great victory.

SHAKA
The Butelezi were a field of grain, and the Zulu army swept down like a great cloud of locust and covered the sun. We ate them up until not one stalk was left standing.

NANDI

The drums have been roaring your deeds from the mountaintops. I have been waiting to hear of your exploits from your own lips.

SHAKA

Would you have me approach you before I cleansed the ax?

NANDI

You have been long enough about it.

SHAKA

(Tenderly.)

You are always impatient for my return. Be still, woman, I am here now.

NANDI

You have a harem of maidens, and yet you lie with only one while the rest languish. It is not right to break with tradition this way.

SHAKA

A warrior has no time for dalliance with a harem of prattling women. Would you have me grow weak with their entreaties?

NANDI

What good are a mother's words? When children are small, they suckle our milk. When they are older, they eat our hearts.

SHAKA

Listen to me, Mother. I cannot rest until I have made a wall around our people to protect them from their enemies. Already the white tribes from across the great ocean have taken our shores. When they move north, we must be ready for them.

NANDI

The white tribes from across the ocean? Those pitiful termites would never dare move against your armies. You would crush them with one blow.

SHAKA
They are not as helpless as you suppose. A great storm always begins with a few drops of rain. The Zulu must be a powerful nation, united against our enemies. If we weaken we will go under.

NANDI
Then you should have a dozen wives, big with child, like every great chief. You will need many sons who will support your cause. Where are they?

SHAKA
My father had sons. They could hardly wait to seize his power.

NANDI
Why should I try to talk to you? You never listen to my advice anymore. Pampata would be the only one to bear you a son. She has cast a spell over you.

SHAKA
So that's it. Still your jealous tongue. You have my heart as always. I went into battle with your name and have brought you the victory.

NANDI
I see that you could hardly wait to present it to me.

SHAKA
Enough, I said! I will not be caught between two women. That is a battle no man can win. I need a bath, not idle words.

NANDI
(To her SERVING WOMAN.)
Did you not hear? Go quickly. Don't stand there gaping! And see that the water is just at the right temperature!
(SERVING WOMAN exits. NANDI to SHAKA.)
I have prepared all the dishes that you like. But first I will see to your comfort and scrub your back. These women can't be trusted to do anything right.

SHAKA

If you care for my comfort, woman, go and prepare my food. I trust no one but you to flavor it just to my liking. I am hungry as a lion with a fresh kill.

NANDI

Go then, and rest, and all will be prepared with my own hands.

SHAKA

You will hear more of the battle presently.

> (HE exits.)

NOBELA

> (Comes out of the hut where she has been listening. SHE speaks in a whining voice.)

He treats an old woman with contempt. He would twist my neck like a chicken when I am no longer useful to him. It is dangerous to challenge the powers of darkness.

NANDI

The young are impatient and think they know everything. Serve me and my wishes, and while I live you will live and grow fat. Keep him alive and unharmed.

NOBELA

All of your wishes will come true, oh Queen. Did you not wish that the Old Chief would sicken and die as if from old age?

NANDI

Do not speak of that deed again! You were well paid for that. Speak of the future.

NOBELA

I threw the bones in the smoke and saw many things. All your wishes will come true. You have but to speak.

NANDI

Pampata's death would please me well. Have it done so that no suspicion falls on me and I will pay you a king's ransom.

NOBELA

Pampata's cord would be cut as easily as the neck of a chicken. But do you wish your son's death, also?

NANDI

Stop your mouth, you evil hag! He is the breath of life to me.

NOBELA

Then she must live. Their lives hang by the same cord. Even I cannot change that. They will live and die together. I have seen it in the smoke.

NANDI

So be it then. But see that he never takes her as his wife and that she has no son of his that will make her name greater than my own in his heart. Perhaps if she gives him no sons, he will tire of her.

NOBELA

Then it is done.

NANDI

Do not betray me. Remember, while I live, you will live.

NOBELA

Then live and grow great, oh Queen.
    (SHE bows as NANDI exits.)
But beware of what you wish, oh Queen, for wishes are deeds that bear strange fruit.

END OF SCENE FOUR

ACT I: SCENE FIVE

(NARRATOR enters the bare stage. SOUND of DRUMS.)

NARRATOR

Shaka united all the scattered tribes from the mountains to the sea. He made the Zulu a great people. Where he walked, the earth trembled. When he raised his spear, the rivers ran with blood. His enemies fell before him, like grain before the storm. In victory after victory, nothing could defeat him.

(The DRUMS INCREASE. ALL enter the stage for the victory celebration. As SHAKA takes his place on the raised seat of the Great Chief with NANDI to his right and PAMPATA to his left, the CROWD thunders his name.)

CROWD

Bayete! Shaka Zulu! Bayete! Shaka Zulu! Bayete! Shaka Zulu!

(At a gesture from SHAKA, MGOBOZI steps forward.)

MGOBOZI

Where is the praise singer who will sing his name?
His roar was as thunder across the plain.
Lion among men was our lord this day.
On the field of battle he seized his prey.
Sharp is his tooth and sharp his claw.
We fought by the Lion's mighty law.

(A YOUNG WARRIOR dances a traditional dance of SHAKA, the Lion. As the dance ends, a MAIDEN steps forth. The DRUMS take a different beat.)

MAIDEN

The earth longs for the rain.
The blossoms long for the sun.
All night I cry
For the rain to come.
All night I cry
For my lover to come.
The wind in the trees whispers of rain.
Come, my love, make me fruitful again.
Come, my love, make me fruitful again.

YOUNG WARRIOR

Here is my seed, in your warm earth.
Here is my seed, waiting for birth.

(The MAIDEN and YOUNG WARRIOR dance opposite each other in a traditional dance of fertility and renewal. As the dance ends, DINGANE steps forth and addresses SHAKA.)

DINGANE

Live, oh Great Chief, son of a great father, scourge of the Butelizi, Great Lion whose roar makes all tremble. We celebrate your victory.

(HE bows and retires.)

NANDI

We celebrate the harvest, our victory over starvation and death. As you harvest our enemies that the Zulu may live. You have cut down the dry stalks and we have stored the grain.

MBOPA

Live and grow great, Oh King. The time of harvest has come when warriors choose their wives that they may be fruitful as the land is fruitful. That their womb may grow full as the moon is full and bear a bountiful harvest. That they may honor the ancestors with many children to praise their name.

(SHAKA rises slowly and majestically. He is silent while all becomes still; everyone is waiting expectantly.)

SHAKA

I have said that my word will be your new law. Nothing of the past will stand if it does not serve me. Children obey their parents. That is the law of the Zulu. You are my children, and I am your father.

MBOPA

Give us your blessing. May you bear many sons, oh King, and live forever.

NOBELA

(Steps forth and addresses SHAKA.)

Oh, wise ruler! Oh, Great King! Bravest of warriors! Lead us, oh Father, for we are you children. The ancestors guard your tongue. They have spoken to me in the dead of night. Harken to my words. A wise chief must beware of sons who bear his name. They are a sharp spear waiting for the moment to strike. He who has ears, let him hear.

(DINGANE is alarmed by her words, but SHAKA takes no notice.)

SHAKA

I will have no sons to hold a spear at my throat.

NANDI

Your words fall on willing ears, oh Mother of Darkness.

SHAKA

Listen and obey my words. From this day, only the strongest and bravest among my warriors will take wives and bear children.

MBOPA

(To SHAKA.)

The seed must be planted or there is no harvest and the people will die. Who can turn the course of nature, oh Great Chief?

SHAKA

(To MBOPA.)

Do we not choose the strongest bull to mount our heifers and bear strong calves? The scrawny steers go to the slaughter.

(To the CROWD.)

No warrior will take a wife until he has proved again and again in the heat of battle that he is fit to father a new generation of warriors. No warrior will take a wife, no children will be born without my permission. The child born without my blessing will die. I have spoken.

MBOPA

(To SHAKA.)

What you have spoken is against tradition.

SHAKA

Listen, old man, I have said that I am tradition. My word has been spoken. Have I not kept the people safe from their enemies?

(To the CROWD.)

Have I ever asked you to go into battle and I not taken the first blow?

WARRIORS

Bayete!

SHAKA

When you trampled the field of battle, did I not lead the way and show you how to dance?

WARRIORS

Bayete!

SHAKA

When you were thirsty, did I alone drink?

WARRIORS

Bayete!

SHAKA

When you were hungry, did I eat and let you starve?

WARRIORS

Bayete!

SHAKA

Where have I asked you to go that I did not lead? I am your king, but I will have no wife and she will bear no sons until my people are safe. I need no other sons.

> (PAMPATA, unnoticed by anyone, draws away from SHAKA and turns and exits.)

ALL

Bayete! Shaka Zulu! Bayete!

SHAKA

Now I will show you how loyalty and bravery are rewarded.
> (To NOBELA.)

He who has ears, let him hear.
> (To the WARRIORS.)

Where is Mzilikazi?
> (MZILIKAZI, a handsome young warrior, steps forward.)

When the horns of the crescent closed about the enemy, he was the first to lead the charge. He reminds me of myself when I was young, full of fire and ready for battle. He will continue under my special notice, for I see greatness in him. He will be raised from the ranks and given a new command.

MZILIKAZI

Bayete! Oh, Great Lion! Bayete!

SHAKA

Who among you was the great shield that covered my back?

                        WARRIORS
Mgobozi!

                         SHAKA
Who is your favorite? Bravest of brave warriors to follow his king?

                        WARRIORS
Mgobozi!

           (THEY good-naturedly push MGOBOZI forward.)

                         SHAKA
                  (Grasping MGOBOZI'S arm.)
Oldest of friends. Bravest of warriors. My good right arm. Brave heart who laughs in the teeth of death. You are my brother on the field of battle.

                        MGOBOZI
It is easy to follow a brave king who takes the heaviest blow first. Even cubs are safe with the lion about.

                         SHAKA
And ever a ready tongue. If he has one fault it is that he is too magnanimous to the enemy and pleads mercy for the defeated. How many wounds have you taken in my place?

                        MGOBOZI
Where do you think I got this ugly face, oh king, that makes the maidens turn away in fright? I was scarred by the spears meant for you.

                         SHAKA
The maidens look lower down to another spear and are better pleased. I have seen their glances in that direction.
           (To the WARRIORS.)
This is the warrior who will father Zulu sons. He will be well rewarded for his bravery.
                   (To MGOBOZI.)

In celebration of our victory and the harvest, I have chosen twenty of the most beautiful maidens for your wives. Look, here is a sample of the choicest fruit of the harvest.
>(HE gestures, and a lovely MAIDEN, obviously pleased, steps forward.)

Does she please you?

MGOBOZI

One such treasure and I am a wealthy man. But twenty brides—how can I pay such a bride price?

SHAKA

I have set the price myself. You will forfeit one goat from your herd for each day a bride remains unsatisfied and unconsummated.

VOICES from the CROWD
>(Jokingly.)

You will make a beggar of him.
He will lose his entire herd with such a bargain.
His spear will drop to the ground and never rise again.

MGOBOZI
>(Answering joke for joke.)

Not one goat will be lost. You will see. My strength will be equal to the task.

NANDI

Remember, Mgobozi, men boast today, but women will gossip tomorrow.

MGOBOZI

They will be too full of praise, oh Queen, to gossip long. They will be longing for the night.

SHAKA

Prepare for your wedding day, old friend. You will need all the rest you can get.

MGOBOZI

Keep an eye on my goats while I am away. I will count them when I return. I vow: Not one goat will be lost or one bride unsatisfied.

SHAKA

(To MBOPA.)

See that the forfeit comes from my own herds. I know Mgobozi well. He and his brides will spend one whole night laughing at his jokes and the next in conversation. Then as if confronting the enemy, he will show each bride such prolonged "mercy" that his whole herd will be consumed in the process.

(To the CROWD.)

Let there be feasting and dancing. To each regiment a hundred head of cattle. We wish our old friend joy in his wedding and many sons. Pampata and I will name your first-born son.

(HE turns to discover PAMPATA has gone. DRUMS INCREASE. ALL leave the stage.)

END OF SCENE FIVE

ACT I: SCENE SIX

(A clearing. From stage left SHAKA enters with his retainers and from stage right PAMPATA enters with her serving women. They stand looking at each other.)

SHAKA
(Gestures for HIS RETAINERS to leave. THEY exit.)
Dismiss your women.
(PAMPATA gestures, and the women exit.)
Where have you been, woman?

(HE points at HER in anger.)

PAMPATA
Did you send for me, my lord?

SHAKA
Why did you insult our old friend, Mgobozi, by leaving?

PAMPATA
I meant no insult to Mgobozi. I do not think he noticed my absence among his twenty brides. He was too busy celebrating victory and future sons. But I had no cause to celebrate.

SHAKA
If your father had not been a true foster father to me and ever a wise councilor, I would have you whipped.

PAMPATA
Do you refrain out of a duty then, or would a whipping scar the flesh you like to nibble?

SHAKA
(Softening HIS tone.)
You are a stubborn woman with a sharp tongue.

(Reaching to touch HER, but SHE pulls away from HIS touch.)

What is it? I know you. When something troubles you, your body grows distant, and your spirit withdraws deep inside itself. Do you think you can fool me?

PAMPATA

Have I ever tried to fool you?

SHAKA

No, I can always look to you for the truth when everyone else speaks with a lying tongue. A man needs one councilor he can trust.

PAMPATA

Mgobozi is your oldest friend. You can trust him.

SHAKA

Yes, but his mind is straightforward and guileless as a child. He lives only for the moment. You see the beginning and the end.

PAMPATA

Your mother would give her life for you. Can you not trust her?

SHAKA

She plays her own game, always. She thinks she knows what is best for me and behind my back will pursue her own ends. You are the other half of my spirit. My most valued advisor. I trust you above all others.

(HE reaches to touch HER.)

Have I ever left you unsatisfied? You scratch my back like a leopard and then afterwards moan softly like a turtle dove. You are well served if I am any judge of women.

PAMPATA

You make me melt with pleasure like warm honey in the sun.

SHAKA
And yet you are not satisfied. What more do you want, woman?

PAMPATA
You have given me everything—except one thing. Thrust deep inside me, when we lie together. Fill my womb and give me a son.

SHAKA
Now I see which way the wind is blowing. You did not like it when I said I would have no sons.

PAMPATA
What is a woman or a man without sons? An empty house where the wind moans through the dry thatch. One spark, and all is gone, leaving only ashes behind.

SHAKA
The old proverb rings true. Like a bottomless well, women are never filled.

PAMPATA
And men are like arrows. They think they can fly until they are buried in the earth.

SHAKA
Women are like the honeybird. Always they say, "Quick, quick, quick."

PAMPATA
And men are like baobab trees. Always with their heads in the sand.

SHAKA
I have given my word that I will have no sons. Do you think I go back on my word?

PAMPATA
But must I live without sons?

SHAKA

I know that the young bulls think of the old one who rules the herd. I hated my own father and with good cause. If he had not died when he did, I would have risen against him and toppled him from his place. I will have no sons waiting to stab me when my back is turned.

PAMPATA

Then look to your own brothers. They plead illness when you embark on a long campaign. They are waiting for their moment to strike.

SHAKA

They would not have the liver to strike me. They know my spies are everywhere and no one can be trusted. They would not dare climb a tall tree for fear of the height.

PAMPATA

Even a tall tree must be deep rooted in mother earth or be swept away in a storm.

SHAKA

The tree grows tallest that stands alone.

PAMPATA

The tall tree that stands alone draws the lightning.

SHAKA

Then why do you shelter under my branches? If I am struck down, you will fall with me.

PAMPATA

Because—I would rather die with you than live a thousand years.

SHAKA

Then let us have no more harsh words between us. I have dreams of a great Zulu nation that will be feared by all its enemies so that none dare challenge our might. All of my energies must go in that direction.

PAMPATA

All of your strength is spent for the people. You take no thought for yourself.

SHAKA

If we are not strong we will be hiding in the forest, digging for roots with our bare hands to keep from starving, while stronger tribes take our land. I tell you, the white nation from across the sea is already nibbling at our shores. They will not dare to take a great bite of us if the Zulu are strong and stand together. But if we weaken we will be devoured. Those who are not with us are against us. There is no other way.

PAMPATA

But surely your spears are stronger than theirs.

SHAKA

They carry no spears, but a long gun that shoots fiery darts like the blowgun of the little people. Our spears must be a match for their guns. Their numbers are the first wave to touch the shore. Behind it is the great ocean. I intend to show them my friendship and discover the secret of their power. If we can live with respect for each other as men, so much the better. They have their land and we have ours. But if they cross our boundaries they will learn the name of Zulu to their sorrow. If these white men come, I will need your wise council. Help me judge their words. Who can I trust if you are not with me? Stand by me, Pampata.

PAMPATA

Where else would I be if not by your side? There is no other place for me. I am with you, my lord, to the death.

(SHAKA takes her hand, and THEY exit together.)

NARRATOR
(Enters as THEY exit.)
Yes, they are together—for now—but what of his brother, Dingane? Like a leopard in the night, he waits for his moment to strike.

(HE gestures, and Stage LIGHTS DARKEN. SOUND of DRUMS.)

END OF SCENE SIX

ACT I: SCENE SEVEN

(It is night. The same set with the addition of Nobela's conjuring hut and suggestions of a dark forest surrounding the hut. Weird masks hang outside the hut. The SOUND of African FOREST NOISES is heard. DINGANE and MHLANGANA enter from opposite directions, each carrying weapons and looking furtively about. MHLANGANA jumps at every strange noise. DINGANE sees MHLANGANA first and hides behind a tree waiting for HIM. As MHLANGANA passes, DINGANE grabs HIM about the throat and puts a knife to his side.)

MHLANGANA
Ah–h–h–h!

DINGANE
Be still!

MHLANGANA
Dingane?

DINGANE
No names! The trees may be listening. Were you followed?

MHLANGANA
I don't think so. Let me go.
  (DINGANE releases MHLANGANA.)
You drew blood!

DINGANE
I didn't think you had any.

MHLANGANA
What do you mean? I risked my life in coming here.

DINGANE

You have avoided meeting me. Always excuses.

MHLANGANA

His spies are everywhere. Sh–h–h–h!
(Startled.)
What sound is that? The forest is full of demons! I saw their eyes following me.

DINGANE

Fool! They are only animals.

MHLANGANA

I do not like the forest gloom. Why must we meet here?

DINGANE

It was that hyena bitch's idea. No one dares approach her conjuring hut uninvited. We will be safe from prying eyes.

MHLANGANA

She's not to be trusted. She would inform on us if it served her purpose.

DINGANE

True. But I have taken certain precautions.

MHLANGANA

She may be listening.

DINGANE

She could not possibly be here yet.

(ONE of the weird masks outside the hut begins to move.)

MHLANGANA
(Shaking with fear.)

Ah–h–h–h–h!

NOBELA
(From behind the mask, in a cackling voice.)
Welcome, my children. You took the long road. I have been waiting for you.

DINGANE
How did you arrive before me, Mother of Darkness?

NOBELA
I rode my hyena on the back of the wind. We saw you sneaking below us, crawling from shadow to shadow. It made us laugh.

MHLANGANA
She has the evil eye. We are cursed!

DINGANE
Let us not bandy foolish words, Witch Mother. You know why we are here.

NOBELA
You wish a remedy for a certain ailment?

DINGANE
One that will purge us of our ills.

NOBELA
The physic must be carefully prepared and given at the proper time.

MHLANGANA
Does she mean poison? It will never work. He has someone to taste his dishes.

DINGANE
Shut up, you fool!

NOBELA
His tongue is loose. I have a raven would pluck it from his head like a fat worm. Only say the word.

DINGANE
I can handle him. He will keep his mouth shut.

NOBELA
Yes, I know it. You will shut his mouth when the time comes.

DINGANE
Enough of that! I wish to hear of your remedy.

NOBELA
And what of me? When the patient is cured, he has no need of the doctor.

DINGANE
Shaka has branded you a quack. Your powers have been mocked and grow weak with disuse. Cure me, old woman, and your power will be restored. Or would you rather live out your days with empty dugs, laughed at by the village idiot?

NOBELA
Your words sting like the adder and strike true. What is life without power? I have sucked its teat too long to be content with weaker milk.

DINGANE
Then we understand each other.

NOBELA
Be patient. It will take a while. Too hasty brewing would be deadly. I must first plant the hellbane. When it takes root and blossoms, then the brewing can begin.

DINGANE

I will wait for your word.
    (To MHLANGANA.)
Go on ahead.

    (Gestures down another path.)

NOBELA

I would not go that way. A black mamba lies across the path.

MHLANGANA
    (Jumping back.)
She knew that! We could have tred it in the dark!

NOBELA
    (Cackling.)
Had you come that way, it would have been a sign that you were not meant to succeed. But you have passed the test.

DINGANE

Do not play games with me, old woman. I, too, have a deadly sting.

NOBELA

Then we will strike together. Wait for a sign.

    (DINGANE and MHLANGANA exit. BLACKOUT.)

END OF SCENE SEVEN

ACT I: SCENE EIGHT

(NANDI'S royal hut. NANDI is seated on a stool having HER hair arranged by a SERVING WOMAN. NOBELA enters.)

NOBELA

Live and grow great, oh Queen. Your beauty is like the new moon riding in full splendor the distant hills.

NANDI

Is that your only word—that I wax and wane, Mother of Lies? I have been better praised before. Your messenger said the need was urgent.

NOBELA

It is urgent, but for your ears alone. Send your woman away.

NANDI

(Gestures, and the SERVING WOMAN exits.)
What word do you bring me?

NOBELA

Only this.

(SHE holds out a small gourd, its mouth stoppered with wax.)

NANDI

(Looks at the gourd as if in distrust and will not touch it.)
What is this?

NOBELA

A potion for your fondest dreams.

NANDI

Fool! Poison is not the way this time. I would be the first suspected!

NOBELA

This poison takes nine months of darkness and comes forth a living child. Even you cannot be suspected of fathering the results. This holds Pampata's son and your grandson.

NANDI

Has old age coddled your wits? I told you plainly, I do not want that bitch to bear his son. Better she give birth to serpents that would poison her days!

NOBELA

They are one and the same, oh Queen. She will feel the bitter sting.

NANDI

Explain your meaning and do not cloud your words.

NOBELA

This contains a liquid so potent that any man's lust will be fired to fever pitch. His member will swell like a bull in rut and his senses dim. And after, he will remember nothing that has taken place. But she will remember all her days.

NANDI

We both know the Great Lion has said he wants no sons.

NOBELA

But Pampata does. He will not kill Pampata for her disobedience. Their Fate lies together. But it will be the death of trust between them. She will never bear his son again and he will take other women in her stead.

NANDI

But what of this child?

NOBELA

It will surely die. You will see. Convince her that you hold a grandson in your heart and will protect him and her, come what may.

NANDI

But Pampata will never trust me. There is no love lost between us.

NOBELA

You will find the words and soon. I have sent for her in your name.

NANDI

You are very sure of yourself, Mother of Serpents.

NOBELA

The path to power is a slippery way. One learns to be sure footed.

NANDI

How will I convince her?

NOBELA

You will fashion a half-truth that will conceal the whole. I know Pampata. She will never suspect this kind of treachery. Sh–h–h–h. She comes. This must be given when her moon is ripe.

NANDI

(Takes the poison and conceals it.)
Stay hidden until she leaves. I would speak with you again.

(NOBELA conceals herself in an enclosure of animal skins against the wall. PAMPATA is shown into the hut by ONE of the SERVING WOMEN.)

PAMPATA

You sent for me, Mother of the Royal Kraal?

NANDI

(HER back to PAMPATA, NANDI hesitates a moment, then turns to face PAMPATA.)

You have come with better grace than I have ever shown to you.

PAMPATA

I wish to honor the mother of the king.

NANDI

A dutiful thought since I have never honored you. Let us not begin with lies. I have always hated you, and you have hated me.

PAMPATA

If you would have the truth, I do not hate you. That would be the surest way to lose his heart. We are both by his side.

NANDI

I see why he cleaves to you. You are a match for him in spirit and in power. And a fit mother for his sons.

PAMPATA

Ah, there's the hidden knife. Turn it once again and let me go.

NANDI

You mistake my meaning. I know the joy of sons. My breasts have felt their lusty pull. I would have the joy of grandsons to sweeten my old age.

PAMPATA

You have another son who will give you joy.

NANDI

I have only one son who means anything to me.

PAMPATA

Then you and I will share an empty womb. I must beg to be excused. Your knife is buried to the hilt and drains my strength away. Your purpose has been served.

NANDI

(Holds out the potion.)
Take this and choose a son.

PAMPATA

What do you mean?

NANDI

Put this in his drink when your moon is ripe. His lust will rise and will not be denied. You know the place where it will best be satisfied. He will fill you with a son lusty as your dreams. But the potion will be a mist that dims the act to forgetfulness.

PAMPATA

Do you think me that stupid? You would have me be my own executioner.

NANDI

Are you afraid to take the chance? No coward is fit to bear his son.

PAMPATA

Even if I were to agree, Shaka's word is hard as rock and final as the grave.

NANDI

When were men and women ever alike. They are the sun and we the changing moon. They are blazing noon and we the secret night. They are sand and we the yielding sea. They are the storm that passes, but we are the earth that remains. What do men know of the needs of women? Men have their word which they fulfill. But we are the womb of time.

PAMPATA
Yes—in the dark of night, there is no need for words.

NANDI
Let them play their games of spears and war, like little boys. Our womb will create what they destroy. And in the end, it is Mother Earth who receives them back again.

PAMPATA
I see why you have given birth to such a son. But a child is not like a thought that can be concealed. Each passing moon whispers its secret aloud.

NANDI
I have a plan. In the sixth moon, your grandmother who raised you as a child will send for you to tend her ailing years. In filial duty you must go and I will support your cause. There in secret you will give birth and they will guard you and your son and raise the child. When he is older, we will find a way to win his father's heart. You have my word.

PAMPATA
(Suddenly kneels in front of NANDI.)
I will ever honor you in truth if I should bear his son. I will never forget what you have done for me.

NANDI
Yes, see that you remember. That will be the pleasure of my old age. Do not forget what I have done for you.

(SHE places the potion in PAMPATA'S hand, then closes her hand over PAMPATA'S.)

Now take the drug and use it quickly in its strength. We would have no puny sons. Inform me of the results. Go now. I am suddenly tired and old.

(PAMPATA rises and exits. NANDI stands, HER shoulders drooping as if she is tired.)

NOBELA

(Enters from her place of concealment and bows.)
I bow to a master of my craft. Even I began to believe your words. Perhaps the sight of the child will steal your heart.

NANDI

I, too, am hard as stone and final as the grave. I will never look upon its face. But what assurance do I have of the potency of your drug?

NOBELA

I have tested it on my young lovers many times. Ah, how they have proved its potency and used me like the most beautiful of women. I have ached from their embrace. They were my slaves and did whatever I desired.

NANDI

You ugly hag! Hyena's bitch! Get out of my sight! When I look at you I am reminded of my own misshapened thoughts. Be assured, I will guard you well until the act is done. If my son should take harm from this, I will roast you over a slow fire and turn the spit myself. Get out of my sight before I forget the wish that was father to this child.

(NOBELA exits.)

END OF SCENE EIGHT

ACT I: SCENE NINE

(Six months later. SHAKA is preparing for a campaign against his old enemy, Zwide. SHAKA is conferring with MGOBOZI and MZILIKAZI, while a WARRIOR ATTENDANT adjusts the last items of Shaka's war dress. All are dressed for war. NARRATOR stands to one side.)

NARRATOR

Six months later, Shaka prepares a campaign against his old enemy, Zwide, whose kraal is hung with the skulls of chiefs he has defeated. This time Shaka has a new plan to catch the rat in his trap. A half circle of warriors will form on the plain. Once they have Zwide's troops in their firm grasp, the two horns of the crescent will close and the enemy will be circled and ensnared.

SHAKA
(To MGOBOZI.)

Ah, old friend, Zwide will not escape us this time. He will be cornered like the rat he is and his evil mother with him.

MGOBOZI

My men await your review. I have had them under special drill for weeks. They are straining to be off.

MZILIKAZI

Zwide has hidden behind his warriors long enough. This time he will eat earth, I swear it.

SHAKA

Patience, Mzilikazi. You are as impatient as I was at your age. But nothing is accomplished without careful planning. Leave nothing to chance. Check every detail yourself. Prepare your troops. I will review them presently.

MZILIKAZI
Bayete!

(HE salutes with shield and spear and exits.)

SHAKA
As for you, old friend. Perhaps you should have stayed behind on this campaign. Only six of your wives are big with child.

MGOBOZI
They never leave me any peace. I have to go to war to get some rest. It's a hard duty to be married to twenty beautiful women. I will be old before my time. Besides, who will act as your shield against the enemy?

SHAKA
I would sooner have my right arm cut off than not have you to cover my back. We have been through too many campaigns together. Be prepared to march. May the ancestors go with you, old friend.

MGOBOZI
And with you, my lord. Bayete!

(MGOBOZI salutes with shield and spear and exits.)

SHAKA
(To the WARRIOR standing by.)
Check the supplies. See that water is plentiful. Thirst is the worst of enemies on the battlefield.

WARRIOR
Bayete!

(HE exits after saluting. PAMPATA enters.)

PAMPATA
My lord, you are almost ready to leave.

SHAKA

We each go our separate ways. Give your grandmother greetings from me. She was like a grandmother to me when I had few friends.

PAMPATA

She has always held you in her esteem.

SHAKA

Do not worry. The old woman was ever strong. She will keep death at bay a while yet, or I have misjudged her.

PAMPATA

Will your campaign be long?

SHAKA

Zwide is a wily jackal. And has slipped the trap before. It will take a while to set my plan in motion.

PAMPATA

Have you taken leave of your mother?

SHAKA

A short while ago.

PAMPATA

Did she speak to you of me? I sent her word of my grandmother's illness but have received no reply.

SHAKA

My mother is indisposed. A new campaign always leaves her uneasy. But she wishes you a speedy journey, and she said to tell you this: "Eat no strange fruit—the seeds may make you ill." She may be mellowing in her old age. She seemed concerned for you.

PAMPATA
(Anxiously.)
Did she...say anything else? Her exact words.

SHAKA

Only "Be careful what you drink. There are strange poisons that take nine months to work." She said to remind you that no one can be trusted.

PAMPATA
(Visibly shaken.)
Oh, no.

SHAKA

What is it? You're trembling.

PAMPATA

I fear what may come to be.

SHAKA

Have no fear for me. I have come back from many a battle. I am an old campaigner.

PAMPATA
(Looking intently into his eyes.)
Let me look into your eyes once more before you go. Do you remember when first we met?

SHAKA
(Fondly.)
You were a skinny girl with flat breasts.

PAMPATA

And you a lonely herd boy with fiery eyes.

SHAKA

I did not know then how content I was. To sit with the flocks in the silence of the hills, the black silhouette of thorn trees against the sky, and feel the stars turning the great wheel of night.

PAMPATA
You were like no other boy I knew. The fierce, proud look in your eyes. The way you moved with the grace of a leopard about to spring.

SHAKA
And the way you moved with the grace of a gazelle and the proud teasing look you turned my way. We were a match, you and I, proud and set apart from others our age. You grow more beautiful with the passing years and more valued thus to me.

PAMPATA
Everything must end—youth and dreams and power.

SHAKA
What is this strange mood? Is there nothing that will stay?

PAMPATA
Your heart in mine will never pass away. I would not leave your side now, but Fate has sent us separate ways. Do not forget me all that we have shared.

SHAKA
What is it? Have you dreamed of my defeat?

PAMPATA
No. You will win the battle and become the greatest king the Zulu have ever known. No one can defeat you but yourself. But that is the most dangerous enemy of all.

SHAKA
If that were my only enemy, who would need a friend?

PAMPATA
Remember that I have been your friend when we must meet again. Give me your word that you will remember.

SHAKA

I will remember. I give my word. My warriors are waiting and I must go. When we meet again there will be other words between us.

PAMPATA

Yes, there will be other words between us.

SHAKA

Stay well, my sweet gazelle.

PAMPATA

And you—my lord—of lightning and of rain.
> (SHAKA turns and starts to exit. PAMPATA calls to HIM.)

My lord....
> (SHAKA stops and looks back at HER.)

Whatever comes in life or death, I will hold you in my heart.

SHAKA

And you in mine. Be cheerful, Pampata, we will meet again.

> (HE strides offstage quickly as PAMPATA gazes after him. SOUND of DRUMS.)

END OF SCENE NINE

ACT I: SCENE TEN

(Some months later. On the heights above the battlefield on the day after the victorious battle of the Zulus over Zwide and the Ndwandwe forces. SHAKA stands apart in a somber mood. NARRATOR stands to one side of the scene.)

NARRATOR
After a great battle with Zwide and his forces, Shaka is victorious. You must imagine in this circle of firelight 10,000 Zulu spears are gleaming in the sun, awaiting Shaka's command to march home in victory. From this rocky height, Shaka is lord of all that he surveys.

MGOBOZI
(Enters to report.)
Bayete! Oh, Great Chief!

SHAKA
What of Zwide? Has he been found among the dead?

MGOBOZI
The wily jackal has escaped again. He hid in his own kraal when his warriors were hardest pressed and, under cover of the slaughter, escaped into the north.

SHAKA
Send warriors in pursuit. Burn every hut and destroy everything that moves. Zwide must be captured, for like a maggot he breeds best in death and will raise a swarm to sting us once again.

MGOBOZI
Then he will have to raise the dead. His people are food for vultures, and the kites have picked their eyes. They are a broken people and will never rise again.

SHAKA

What of our dead?

MGOBOZI

We lost less than 2,000 men to their 7,000 slain. Look, 10,000 spears stand gleaming in the sun, awaiting your command.

(HE points down and in the distance.)

SHAKA

They are a brave sight. What of the wounded?

MGOBOZI

They have had their wounds dressed and been given healing herbs. Warriors too severely wounded were mercifully dispatched.

SHAKA

They were brave men and died a hero's death. Divide the spoils with the families of the dead when we return. All will have a share.

MGOBOZI

It will be done. The warriors are prepared to march for home to celebrate your great victory.

SHAKA

(In a solemn and pensive mood.)
Celebrate my victory? Then why does it taste so bitter?

MGOBOZI

But you are lord of all that you survey, from the mountains to the sea.

SHAKA

Lord of all that I survey? If that is so, what lands are left to conquer?

MGOBOZI
What enemy could stand against you now?
        (Puzzled, hesitating.)
You act as if great victory were defeat. I cannot guess your mood. What troubles you?

SHAKA
Last night I thought to dream of the victory we have won, but I have had dark dreams that give me troubled thoughts. There is something about to come. I feel it in the air. Listen—can you hear voices in the wind?

MGOBOZI
        (Listening and troubled.)
Only the voice of the wind. You are tired. You were everywhere as if you had a thousand arms. One man cannot do what you have done and not feel the strain.

SHAKA
No, it is more than that. I feel it.

MGOBOZI
What was your dream? Your inyanga will tell you what it means.

SHAKA
I dreamed a raven called my name. And storm clouds boiled with lightning and with rain. Then a great wind covered the land and blew everything away. And voices spoke upon the wind.

MGOBOZI
What did they say?

SHAKA
They were too faint to make it out. Listen—can you hear it now? A voice upon the wind waiting to be born.

        (In the stillness the WIND RISES.)

MGOBOZI
(Listens, then with an effort shakes off the mood.)
It is only the wind. Come, oh, Great Chief, lead your warriors home to their own hearth. The familiar fireside will banish voices and bad dreams.

SHAKA
(Listening.)
Sh–h–h–h–h! I can almost hear it now. It is a name I—once knew. What is it? Can you hear?

MGOBOZI
Only the wind moaning among the hills. Leave this place and lead your warriors' home. This place is—cursed.

SHAKA
There is something in the air.
> (SHAKA turns with blind eyes as if listening to the wind. A shower of blossoms blows across the two men where they stand.)

Look, it is a sign!

MGOBOZI
Strange—blossoms blowing on these rocky heights. Where is the tree?

SHAKA
(Suddenly howls in mortal anguish.)
Ah–h–h–h–h!
> (HE turns suddenly and fixes MGOBOZI with a fierce and terrible look.)

MGOBOZI
(Shaken by the look.)
It means nothing. Only blossoms blowing in the wind.

SHAKA
(In a terrible voice.)
Pampata has betrayed me! I know it!

MGOBOZI
Pampata? She would never betray you!

SHAKA
She has betrayed me, I tell you! I trusted her as I would trust my own mother. And she has betrayed me. Our fate hangs by the same cord. I know it. If she betrays me, it is as if I would betray myself.

MGOBOZI
She would never betray you! These are only phantoms of your troubled dreams with no real substance in the light of day. They will fade like mist before the rising sun.

SHAKA
If my troubled dreams speak true, I will strangle her with my own hands.
(With sudden determination.)
Command the warriors to continue the line of march. Mzilikazi will lead them home. Choose a company and follow me. I go another way. I will not rest until I look into her eyes and know the truth.

MGOBOZI
When you see her, you will laugh at your own fears and regret your troubled thoughts.

SHAKA
She will regret the deed that fathered my distrust and the day that gave birth to my dark thoughts. Prepare to march all night.

(HE strides off stage followed by MGOBOZI.)

NARRATOR
Too late, he will regret the deed that is born on this dark day.

(SOUND of DRUMS. NARRATOR crosses the stage and surveys the scene as the WOMEN assemble in an open space.)

END OF SCENE TEN

ACT I: SCENE ELEVEN

(A few days later. An open space in front of the hut. TWO WOMEN are seated on the ground. FIRST WOMAN comes from the hut and sits with the other two women.)

NARRATOR

In the household of Pampata's grandmother in a distant village, Pampata has given birth to Shaka's son.
(HE exits then returns, greatly agitated.)
The Great Chief comes. The Great Chief himself with many warriors. We are all dead. The ancestors protect us now!

FIRST WOMAN

Quickly! Hide the child!

(SECOND WOMAN quickly enters the hut.)

SHAKA

(Enters with MGOBOZI and a WARRIOR. The FIRST WOMAN falls on hands and knees, HER HEAD bowed down.)
Where is Pampata?
(ALL are afraid to speak.)
Where is she? Speak!

FIRST WOMAN

She is within the hut. She has been ill with fever that almost took her life.

SHAKA

Bring her out!

FIRST WOMAN

She is too ill to walk, oh king. Spare her life.

(CRY of a new babe.)

SHAKA

What child is that?
    (Again, ALL are afraid to speak.)
Speak quickly. I will not ask again.

FIRST WOMAN

It is Pampata's child, oh Great Chief.

SHAKA
(To HIS WARRIOR.)

Drag her out!
    (To MGOBOZI.)
Bring the child!

(The WARRIOR and MGOBOZI enter the hut and return immediately, the WARRIOR dragging PAMPATA by the arm and MGOBOZI tenderly holding the baby wrapped in a covering. The WARRIOR throws PAMPATA at SHAKA'S feet.)

PAMPATA

My lord, I beg you! Hear me!

SHAKA

Slut, you dare to speak and look me in the eyes! You have betrayed me when I trusted you! Where is the man who fathered this child? Name him!

PAMPATA

You don't understand! This is your son! He bears your name and mark. But look into his face and see your own.

SHAKA

I said I would have no sons. I gave my word. When did this act take place?

PAMPATA
I put herbs in your drink, and you forgot yourself in passion. The child is yours! I wanted you to live in him, my lord! Forgive me and look upon your son.

SHAKA
You thought to place your will above mine. All must obey my word. Are you king here that I must bow to you?

PAMPATA
Only look into his face and see your own.

SHAKA
Woman, I have trusted you and you have lied to me.

PAMPATA
No lie. He is yourself new born. He has your head and eyes and is your true son.

SHAKA
I have no sons. I gave my word on that and it will stand. What weakness would I display if I should let this pass? He will die.

PAMPATA
No! No! He is your son! What man does not want sons? But hold him in your arms!

(SHE reaches toward SHAKA in supplication.)

SHAKA
Don't touch me, Woman. No one disobeys me twice. I should have you killed, but I remember other days. But do not touch me.

PAMPATA
Then kill me but spare his life! The disobedience was mine! Let him live! He is your son!

SHAKA

(To MGOBOZI.)

Kill him!

PAMPATA

(Tries to reach the baby, but the WARRIOR restrains HER.)

No! No! Only let me hold him once again. Just once more. My breasts are wet with milk.

SHAKA

(To MGOBOZI.)

Kill him!

MGOBOZI

I will not kill your son and hers while mine are being born. If it must be done, kill the child yourself.

(HE places the covered figure of the baby on the ground between HIMSELF and SHAKA.)

PAMPATA

Oh, let him live! He is your son! Give him your blessing!

SHAKA

(Pauses.)

This is my blessing. He dies!

(HE stabs the covered figure of the child with HIS spear.)

PAMPATA

No!

(Moaning, SHE sinks to the ground, kneeling, HER face to the ground, covering HER head with HER arms.)

SHAKA

Let no one touch her. She belongs to me. If any injure her, they have damaged my property and will feel my anger stir. Leave her there.
      (The WOMEN shrink into the hut.)
Woman, one day you will come crawling on your hands and knees and beg to be forgiven. You will learn who is master here.

      (HE exits followed by WARRIOR. For a moment, MGOBOZI looks at PAMPATA, then he, too, exits.)

      (PAMPATA is left alone on the stage. Wordless, SHE crawls to where the dead CHILD lies and leans over IT. LIGHTS SLOWLY DARKEN to BLACKOUT.)

      END OF SCENE ELEVEN

      END OF ACT I

ACT II: SCENE ONE

(The stage is dark, set with bushes and trees. The distant SOUND of DRUMS is HEARD. The NARRATOR enters.)

NARRATOR

As the years pass and Shaka's power grows, he has become more isolated and alone, trusting no one; distrusting everyone. His word the only law. His reign a reign of terror. Even his women fear him. Like a firestorm in dry grass, his passion consumes each one and passes on. As Shaka's power has grown, so has that of Nobela, who increases her power through the hold she has over Shaka's mother. Pampata now walks alone. She has become a House of Dreams, seeing in dreams a way to heal the people. They know she has the power to comfort and heal.

> (PAMPATA enters. SHE seems thinner and more regal. SHE is dressed in an austere fashion. HER costume, draped over one shoulder, is severe but striking.)

Pampata walks upon the hills, hearing the Voice of the Great Spirit in the wind and in the turning stars.

> (NARRATOR exits. SOUND of DRUMS beating as if a great heart is beating.)

PAMPATA

Oh, Great Spirit, come forth. Guide my dreams. Guide my footsteps on the hills of night. Oh, Great Spirit. I hear your voice on the wind. I listen to your cry. Your voice in the wind and in the turning stars. I feel your great heart beating in the earth. The drums of your pulse beating in my heart. Take my beating heart, it is yours. If it is thy will, take my blood and spill it on the hills.

> (The DRUMS INCREASE in power. Strange, flitting shadows move against the dark. WEIRD SOUNDS of jungle and animal cries begin to fill

the air. What at first we have taken for bushes and trees begin to move and appear as masked and costumed figures dressed like distorted trees and animals which surround PAMPATA, though keeping at a distance. THEY slowly creep menacingly toward her. One of the figures is NOBELA. PAMPATA holds her hands before HER as if she is a sleepwalker or one who is blind, feeling her way. All through the scene PAMPATA is at the center of the movement and never leaves the center until the OTHER FIGURES depart. The OTHER FIGURES move around her.)

PAMPATA

What powers are here that stalk me in the dead of night? I feel your evil breath. Stand forth from behind your mask.

NOBELA

(From the shadows utters a weird cackling sound which starts very high and ends on a low note. It is a wail.)

Wo–o–O–O–O-O.

(Wearing a mask, SHE comes forth from the shadows.)

We are spirits of the night. Dreamers dreaming dreams to wrestle for you soul. Oh, House of Dreams, who dares dispute my power? You dare pit your will with mine. I will destroy you and use you for my ends. You will become my thing to use when I desire.

PAMPATA

We see you, Mother of Foul Deeds. You cannot hide behind a mask. Come forth and show your evil face.

NOBELA

(Removes the mask.)

Here am I. One mask replaces another. Which do you prefer?

PAMPATA
What do you want of me?

NOBELA
Only your spirit and your soul. I stole the clippings from your hair and nails and, mixed with vomit, excrement and bones, I made of them a puppet named Pampata and buried it from the light of day. I bring it out and torture it with thorns, slowly, while I kill a cat that screams. Oh, it gives me pleasure and I thrill upon your pain.

>   (The MASKED FIGURES move closer, threateningly. PAMPATA gestures and the FIGURES stop.)

PAMPATA
What nightmare shapes are these?

NOBELA
These are my children. Their wrists and legs deformed and broken. They are kept in a dark cave and couple with animals and are called to act my unspeakable deeds of darkness. You will be one of them.

PAMPATA
You cannot touch me, Mother of Despair. I feel no pain from you.

NOBELA
You feel no pain? You lie! The night is full of pain. Feel it cracking in the air! Here in the dead of night where spirits walk you are defenseless and alone and will crawl to my command. Look into my eyes and see what you become: ugly, wrinkled, old—howling at the moon against your human lot. Ah–h–h–h–h–h!

>   (SHE howls in true anguish, but PAMPATA remains still and calm.)

I see you as you are.

PAMPATA
Fear turns upon itself. Your spittle poisons your own veins.

NOBELA

I hate you, myself, and all that walk the earth. We claw ourselves to death and call it life. Blood runs streaming down our face, like this and this.

>   (SHE savagely claws HER own face until the blood runs down.)

See your blood. It stains my hands and throat. I'll use it for a charm to snare your life. And you will beg for mercy, but none will hear. Like this: Mercy, Oh, Nameless One! Have mercy! What have I done that I should suffer so? Oh, Nameless One, why do you turn me on a spit and make me burn and burn? Have mercy, Nameless One, and let me die.

PAMPATA

Wake, wake, Mother of Deceit! Your suffering is a dream that tortures you in sleep. You chase your own image in the mist.

NOBELA

>   (Almost insane, gibbering and screaming, pulling out a knife.)

See, see, you begin to beg. I'll have no mercy, but turn the knife like this—

>   (NOBELA stabs HERSELF in the stomach and howls, doubling over in pain.)

—within your guts until you howl. Ah–h–h–h!

>   (SHE falls to her knees and looks up at PAMPATA.)

You will bow to me and weep tears of blood and all to no avail, to no avail.

>   (NOBELA bows her head to the ground, holding her head in her arms as PAMPATA had done at the death of her child. NOBELA rocks from side to side.)

PAMPATA

The past is dead and I have let it go. Your power is all a dream.

NOBELA
No, no—you are defenseless now and will crawl to my command.

(SHE holds out her claw-like hand toward PAMPATA and tries to crawl toward her but collapses on the ground before she can reach PAMPATA, who stands quietly. The MASKED FIGURES fall back from the center as if defeated.)

PAMPATA
(Looking down at NOBELA with neither hate, nor compassion, nor indifference.)

The old woman is tough and strong. She will not die so soon. Take her up, oh Spirits of the night and carry her away. The cock begins to crow.

(The MASKED FIGURES lift NOBELA as if she were dead and carry her away in solemn ritual. PAMPATA turns her back and walks in the opposite direction. All exit. LIGHTS SLOWLY COME UP on stage as SPOT FADES.)

END OF SCENE ONE

ACT II: SCENE TWO

(SOUND OF DRUMS. LIGHT COMES UP on stage. A small hut UC within a grove of trees and bushes. The hut is in the hills, set apart from the rest of the village. TWO MESSENGERS are hidden in the foliage.)

PAMPATA
(SHE enters from stage Right. SHE carries a basket on one arm and walks with her head up. As she approaches the hut, she pauses, very still, but without turning. She has her back to the TWO MESSENGERS.)

What do you want of me?

(TWO MESSENGERS come out of hiding.)

SECOND MESSENGER
The Great King has sent us and commands that you appear.

PAMPATA
(Places her basket on the ground without replying. Without looking at the TWO MESSENGERS, SHE, at last, speaks.)

Tell him I have become a House of Dreams and must obey their call. It is not what I would choose but have been chosen.

SECOND MESSENGER
He has heard that you wander on the hills and speak with the ancestors in your dreams. But he commands that you appear. It is a royal decree.

FIRST MESSENGER
He will kill us if you do not obey.

PAMPATA

Tell him I obey an earlier command. That no one touch me until I crawl on hands and knees to beg his favor once again. Tell him I live under that decree and his word is law.

FIRST MESSENGER

We do not dare. He will have us killed and you.

PAMPATA

He has killed me once before. In this land, I grow used to death. It is my familiar spirit. Tell him that from me.

SECOND MESSENGER

Give us a charm to turn his wrath away, or we are dead men.

PAMPATA

(Looking at THEM intently.)

Your fate is charm enough. I read it in your face. It is not your time to die. Go and have no fear. He seeks another kill.

> (The TWO MESSENGERS bow in awe and touch the hem of HER garment and retreat in fear. THEY exit. SHE kneels by the basket once again, sorting herbs. SHAKA steps quietly from HIS place of concealment. He stands looking at her. She raises her head without looking at him. Then slowly she stands and turns in his direction. They look at each other.)

SHAKA

Is this what you've become: an empty house filled with dreams?

PAMPATA

Is this what you've become: a lion that eats men?

SHAKA

Or be eaten. A king must rule by power or fall. There is no other choice.

PAMPATA
It is a lonely path you walk

SHAKA
I would have you with me in the night. It would be less lonely then.

PAMPATA
You can force me. You have said you rule by power. You are the king and can command.

SHAKA
What good is a woman forced? Flesh without spirit is an empty thing. I want your spirit to match my own and hear you moan beneath me once again.

PAMPATA
It is growing late. The spirits speak to me in the night of time and change. All things must have an end.

SHAKA
Then let it end! Why should I bow to you? You look older and there are lines around your mouth and eyes. I have a hundred women with unlined cheeks and firm breasts. Why do I need you?

PAMPATA
You have said it. Why do you need me? What more is there to say? Your women are waiting for your return.

SHAKA
Don't pretend with me! I know you from long ago. You cannot forget what we have been or turn your heart away.

PAMPATA
I could sooner stop the seasons in their flight than turn my heart away.

SHAKA

You are the other half of my soul, Pampata. Come back and be as we were.

PAMPATA

Come back and be as we were? Where would that place be? The past is gone and our son is dead. There is no past. It was all a dream. We dreamers learn of dreams.

SHAKA

One last time. Will you come? I will not ask again.

>   (HE looks at HER for a long moment then starts to turn away.)

PAMPATA

You have many enemies. Be on your guard. It is dangerous to walk alone. Nobela seeks your power.

SHAKA

The old spider will be trapped in her own web. She controls the tribes with superstitious fear. But they hate her. Let her once slip and they will turn against her and tear her to pieces. I will deal with her.

PAMPATA

There is a mightier enemy than she. Beware.

SHAKA

Who is he? Tell me his name!

PAMPATA

Shaka, the Lion, who stalks the land and rules by fear and death. He is your enemy and grows more fierce with each passing day.

SHAKA

We all have such an enemy. The shadow that walks with us. That is the greatest battle still to come, to meet him face to face. All others are shadows of that shadow. Will you stand with me or against me when that time comes?

PAMPATA

I will stand with you when that time comes.

SHAKA

Then, we will meet again, you and I.

PAMPATA

Yes, we will meet again, you and I.

>(THEY look at each other for a long moment. SHAKA strides off stage while PAMPATA looks after him.)

END OF SCENE TWO

ACT II: SCENE THREE

(Night. The Royal Kraal. SOUND of DRUMS RISING in intensity. BLUE LIGHTS, suggesting night, RISE DIMLY, but enough for the stage to bee seen. MALE FIGURE enters. HE is wearing the mask of a bull. Filmy red scarves are attached to his body. As HE dances the desecration of the Royal Kraal, he throws the red scarves about the stage. The FIGURE smears the kraal with the blood of the royal bull then exits. LIGHTS UP.)

NARRATOR
(Entering.)
Call the guards! Someone has killed the king! Help! Help! Guards! Guards!

(TWO GUARDS enter running, carrying spears and shields at the ready.)

FIRST GUARD
Stand where you are. My spear is at your heart.

SECOND GUARD
What outcry is this? You will wake the king!

NARRATOR
The royal bull is killed. Speared and its throat cut. See, the bloody trail leads here!

SECOND GUARD
What deed is this? The kraal is smeared with blood.

NARRATOR
Murder! Someone has killed the king!

FIRST GUARD
Impossible! We stood guard all night!

SECOND GUARD
No one could pass our spears!

NARRATOR
Only witchcraft! Desecration and witchcraft!

FIRST GUARD
(To the SECOND GUARD.)
See if the king still lives.

SECOND GUARD
If he lives, we are dead men. He will make us pay.

(HE starts towards the Royal Hut. SHAKA suddenly enters. NARRATOR and GUARDS fall back in terror. GUARDS salute with spears against shields.)

SHAKA
What noise is this? Who dares disturb my rest?

NARRATOR
Oh, Mighty King, the royal bull is dead, speared and its throat slit! The bloody trail leads here!

SHAKA
Blood is everywhere. Who has dared insult my name? Answer!

FIRST GUARD
Oh, Great King, no one could pass the gates. We guarded them all night.

SHAKA
You slept and let this deed be done!

SECOND GUARD
Oh, Great King, we swear by your name and by our sister's name; we never closed our eyes.

FIRST GUARD
Have mercy, oh Great King, no one passed the gates.

NARRATOR
It was witchcraft! Witchcraft is invisible.

SHAKA
(In contempt.)
Witchcraft? By my name, someone will pay for this. Follow the trail! See where it leads.

NARRATOR
It is here, there, everywhere! Then vanishes into thin air.

SHAKA
(To the FIRST GUARD.)
Arouse the Royal Guards. Find the desecrater of my house. Smell him out. His hands are smeared with blood. He must be found. Alert the kraal.

(FIRST GUARD exits, followed by SECOND GUARD and the NARRATOR. SHAKA exits. SOUND OF DRUMS.)

END OF SCENE THREE

ACT II: SCENE FOUR

(DINGANE and NOBELA enter.)

DINGANE
Is this your witchcraft? Will my brother and I be next or be suspected?

NOBELA
You were far away. You have witnesses to that—or so you say.

DINGANE
We must escape while there is still time.

NOBELA
And point the finger of blame at us. No! Unless— you are guilty of the crime?

DINGANE
You are the guilty one, hyena's bitch!

NOBELA
Fool! Do you think I would slit my own throat?

DINGANE
I warn you. If we fall, you will go down with us.

NOBELA
You and your brother are both fools! Your hasty action has destroyed all my plans. We are all in danger now!

DINGANE
Old Hag, don't smear us with your blood! I see the game you play. We will not be your scapegoat and let you slit our throats. The blame will point your way. I'll see to that. We won't die alone!

NOBELA

Wait—now I see the truth. I am not blind. Who did this has played into our hands. We'll not lose the advantage now. I will declare a smelling out, and by the law I will place the blame. The power has passed to us, and we must not let it drop. Listen to my plan.

DINGANE

Why should I trust you?

NOBELA

Because you have no choice.

DINGANE

What is your plan? Tell me now. I do not choose to stumble in the dark into a trap staked by you.

NOBELA

Listen then. This is our chance to condemn those closest to the king. Mgobozi, Mzilikazi, and others must fall and leave the Old Lion with his back against the wall.

DINGANE

Are they the guilty ones?

NOBELA

I choose the guilty in a smelling out. When I make the choice, the mob will follow me.

DINGANE

His friends will beg clemency of the king.

NOBELA

A sharpened stake driven into the guts leaves little time for talk. Be cautious. Your time of greatness is almost here.
    (SHE gestures.)
Go now. We must not be seen together.
    (DINGANE exits. NOBELA, tearing at HER hair,

acts the part of shocked discovery.)
Desecration! Desecration of the king's name!

>   (DRUMS RISE. NOBELA, Taking Center stage, throws dust upon HER hair and rips HER garments.)

Desecration! Desecration of the king's name! Pollution and witchcraft are everywhere!

MBOPA
(Enters.)
What must be done to free us of this curse?

>   (PEOPLE enter.)

NOBELA
There must be a smelling out to clear the air of foul pollution or we are dead! Death and famine everywhere!
>   (SHE gestures toward the audience as if they are part of the crowd.)

Your babeS will droop and sicken in your arms and die. Men will starve and eat their brothers' corpseS. Vultures, vultures will feed upon our flesh! Witchcraft is here! I smell it in the air. Desecration! Desecration of the king's name!

>   (SHAKA appears followed by NANDI.)

MBOPA
Oh, Great Chief, the people have come before you in terror and in fear. Protect us now.

>   (SHAKA and NANDI take their places UC. DINGANE enters at Stage Right and stands near the NARRATOR. MGOBOZI and MZILIKAZI enter at Stage LEFT and stand near SHAKA.)

SHAKA

Nobela has spoken. There must be a smelling out to find those responsible for the blood. The royal bull was mine, symbol of my strength and power. No one dares touch it but the king. I will be avenged of this and restore my power this day.

NANDI

(Alarmed, aside to SHAKA.)

Beware, my son. I am afraid of her. Do not trust Nobela. She means you harm.

NOBELA

(Overhearing NANDI'S words.)

Oh, Mother of the Great King. Ever the king's loyal support. Give him your advice. I know full well your loyalty to the king. I know your many deeds that have smoothed his way to greatness. With such a mother, oh king, who would not be great. She will support you and me in this and condemn those that I condemn, the enemies of your name. If you but knew how loyal she has been and worked in your behalf. I should tell you all that she has done. But let her modesty speak for itself. I will not betray her now. I lead a smelling out to glorify your name!

MBOPA

The King must be avenged. Let Nobela speak and we will execute the guilty.

SHAKA

So be it, by my decree. But before the people, I solemnly declare.
(Points to NOBELA.)
Do not slip in this. He who swears falsely will be seized and take the victim's place. I will know who are my friends and who my enemies are. I will not be deceived again. The people, too, will know who has spoken truth and who has lied. Be forewarned. I have spoken and stand by my word. Find the guilty one or you will die.

(DRUMS begin to beat. NOBELA calls forth TWO masked SORCERERS. ALL retreat in terror leaving the masked SORCERERS at stage CENTER to dance the smelling-out. NOBELA wields a jet black fly whisk that acts like a baton directing the weird dance of the SORCERERS. As the dance ends, NOBELA circles menacingly toward the king and HIS FRIENDS. SHAKA makes a protective gesture and HIS FRIENDS draw closer to his side. The DRUMS INCREASE in intensity. NOBELA appears to approach the king. In a lightning movement she leaps past the SORCERERS and strikes MGOBOZI and MZILIKAZI and then leaps back to the protection of the SORCERERS. MGOBOZI and MZILIKAZI stand back to back with spears ready to strike the SORCERERS as the SORCERERS approach. SHAKA gestures to stop them. NOBELA suddenly stops at CENTER stage and points at SHAKA and then at MGOBOZI and MZILIKAZI. The DRUMS CEASE abruptly. A hush falls over the CROWD. For an instant there is a tableau where ALL are still.)

NOBELA
These are the guilty ones, oh King, who called themselves your friends. These are the ones with blood upon their hands who hoped to seize your power.

MGOBOZI
Your foul mouth pollutes the air with lies!

MZILIKAZI
(With a threatening gesture toward NOBELA.)
I'll cut out her lying tongue before I die!

(NOBELA is protected by HER SORCERERS.)

NOBELA

They are the source of foul pollution and have desecrated your kraal. They must die before it can be cleansed. They must die or else all will suffer for their deeds.

MGOBOZI
(To SHAKA.)

I have been your loyal shield and covered your back in many a battle. Would you believe her lies?

SHAKA

Do you accuse my oldest friends?

NOBELA

The king must obey his law, else by what law is there a king? You must send them to their deaths. Kill them! Kill them!

(The SORCERERS move forward in response.)

SHAKA
(Restrains THEM with a gesture.)

Stop!

NOBELA
(SHE turns on SHAKA.)

The law demands their life, for their shame is naked in our sight! They must die! I have spoken!

SHAKA
(Addressing NOBELA.)

You have spoken? Are you the King? You but accuse; I pronounce judgment on the guilty according to the law. They will die who prove false to me. Before the people, Oh, Mother of Lies, once again solemnly declare who are the guilty ones.

NOBELA
(Pointing to MGOBOZI and MZILIKAZI.)

There! There! Can you not see your friends who stand before you? Those are the guilty ones who stink of blood! I have the power to smell them out! The ancestors speak to me in dreams. "Seize Mgobozi!" they said, " or we can n'er be clean! Seize Mzilikazi and revenge our house and name! We give the power to you!"

> (SHE turns to the CROWD and points at them as if attacking each one.)

When they spoke to me in dreams, I trembled and shook with fear, as you are shaking now. I stand between you and their fearful words to protect you in their name.

SHAKA

Nobela has spoken. Now I will speak. Hear me now, your King, who protects you in my name. I will charge the guilty ones and they will die who prove false to me.

> (HE points at MGOBOZI and MZILIKAZI as if to accuse them.)

Mgobozi and Mzilikazi have been loyal friends, but now they stand accused. Those who would betray me must die.

PAMPATA
(Suddenly enters from stage LEFT.)

Wait! I have not spoken yet. I am a House of Dreams and have the right to speak and accuse the guilty ones.

SHAKA

Be careful what you say. You have no part in this. I know the truth. He who speaks falsely to me will die. I have given my word and even you will not be safe. There is no need for you to speak.

PAMPATA

But I will speak the truth before the people and the king. Mgobozi was my friend. I have the right to speak and will be heard.

SHAKA

The blood be on your head. I wash my hands of it.

PAMPATA

You cannot remove the stain. For I accuse the King.
(SHE points directly at SHAKA.)
The blood is on his hands. He killed the royal bull and smeared the kraal with blood.

(ALL gasp in astonishment and fall back from the king. The silence is full of suspense.)

NOBELA

Fool! He will have you killed for this!

SHAKA
(Looking directly at NOBELA.)
I do not kill those who speak the truth, but you will die. This was a test to separate false diviners from the true. I said I would know who are my friends and who my enemies are. And now the people know and see your claws and stripe.
(HE addresses the CROWD.)
Only the king dare touch the royal bull. With my own hands, I killed him and smeared the kraal with blood to test Nobela and her crew. No one seizes my power. She thought to ensnare me in a trap and is caught by her own hand. Seize her!

(NOBELA tries to escape but is stopped by the SORCERERS.)

SHAKA

She is a wily serpent. Guard her close, lest she escape again.
(To NOBELA.)
Mother of Hyenas, you will die a lingering death caged with a hungry member of your tribe. He will slowly devour you bit by bit when you are too weak to fend him off. See if your lies will avail you then against his slavering jaws.

NOBELA
(Suddenly cackles a high, mad laugh.)
So you have won, oh King. We'll see.
(SHE puts something into HER mouth.)
Before I die I will speak the truth that will make you wish for death. Do you think I cannot see what is to come, blind though it is in mist and smoke? The ancestors speak to me and trouble me with dreams. But who would believe my words? Men feed on lies and vomit up the truth, too foul for them to bear. I see the future now before my inner eye played out as if it were the past.
(In a trance like state SHE turns and points to MZI-LIKAZI.)
Mzilikazi, your foster son, will desert you. He but waits his chance to lead a tribe and will challenge your power and name. He seeks fame greater than your own.

MZILIKAZI
Hyena's Bitch! I'll turn the skewer in your guts and watch you die!

NOBELA
Act quickly then, Traitor.
(SHE points to MGOBOZI.)
Mgobozi, you will die in your next battle and leave Shaka friendless and alone. I thought this was that battle, but it will come. But have no fear, Mgobozi, you'll die a hero's death, and your name will live as long as there is a Zulu to sing your praise.

MGOBOZI
I'll meet you on the field of death and settle old scores.

NOBELA
I'll go before and wait for you.
(SHE points to DINGANE.)
Your brothers will seize their time or take it with a spear and then turn and rend each other.

DINGANE

She lies! Kill her now!

NOBELA
(Looking at PAMPATA but speaking to SHAKA.)

Pampata will not die until your time has come. And at the last, she will follow you to death in the name of life.

(PAMPATA stands looking at NOBELA but does not give ground. NOBELA turns to NANDI.)

And your mother, who loyally stands by your side. She has betrayed you time and time again. She killed your father and your son to hold you in her power. She poisoned your father and let that poison work in you so that you killed your own son. She could not bear that one stood at your side more dear to you than she. Mother of Lies? She is the master there. I bow to one more full of serpent skill than I.

(NANDI seems on the point of collapse. NOBELA points to SHAKA.)

And you, oh King, great and mighty lord, whose voice shakes the world, whose word is life and death. All you have done will run through your hands like sand and vanish into dreams.

(As if dazed, SHE looks at HER own hands.)

All you have done will run through your hands like sand and vanish into dreams.

(SHE slowly sinks to the ground, her body leaning forward into her hands.)

SHAKA

Seize her! Who would believe her now. Mother of Lies, she will die choking on her words.

ONE of the SORCERERS
(Starts to seize NOBELA, but when he touches her, she falls over dead.)

She is dead.

SHAKA

Slippery as ever, the old serpent has escaped. She was a fierce warrior who battled to the end. Place her body among her tribe; the hyenas and the vultures will give her burial.

(NANDI suddenly collapses to the ground. PAMPATA rushes to HER side and kneels beside HER.)

PAMPATA

Your mother, oh King, cannot be roused.

SHAKA

Take her away. The test is done.

(ALL exit. DRUMS SOUND. BLACKOUT.)

END OF SCENE FOUR

ACT II: SCENE FIVE

(NANDI'S hut. Outside the hut and to the RIGHT a WARRIOR stands guard, holding a spear. Inside the hut, NANDI is lying on a low couch attended by PAMPATA and a SERVING WOMAN.)

NANDI

My son—where is he?

PAMPATA
(At NANDI'S side.)
I have sent for him. Rest, be still. He will come.

NANDI

I must speak to him before I die. Beg that he forgive. I did it all for him.

PAMPATA

Sh–h–h, I know. He will be here.

NANDI

He hates me now.

PAMPATA

No, he could never hate you.

NANDI

I never held a grandson in my arms and now it is too late. I killed your son. Now who will mourn when I am gone?

PAMPATA

Your son will mourn.

NANDI

We will both die and leave nothing of the past. No sons to carry on our name. I am afraid of the endless night with no descendants to call to in the lonely dark. Send for my son.

PAMPATA

I have. Sh–h–h , he will come.
(To the SERVING WOMAN.)
Send for him again. Tell him his mother calls his name.

(SERVING WOMAN starts to exit. SHAKA enters. SERVING WOMAN bows to the ground. PAMPATA sees HIM and goes to HIS side.)

SHAKA

How is she?

PAMPATA

Resting somewhat now. But she is very ill. She has called and called your name. Forgive her.

SHAKA

I will never forgive her. She betrayed me.

PAMPATA

She is paying with her life.

(SHE motions to the SERVING WOMAN, who follows as PAMPATA exits.)

NANDI

(Stirring restlessly, then opening her eyes, becoming aware that SHAKA has entered.)
I have been dreaming that you were here. Are you here or is it still a dream?
(HE crosses to her side.)
Yes, it is you. I see your angry frown. Forgive me. You must forgive me before I die.

SHAKA

There is nothing to forgive. You have taught me an important lesson. No one can be trusted. I have learned that lesson well. It's one I won't forget.

NANDI

No talk of forgiveness then. Let me hold you in my arms once more as I did when you were young. In dreams you're always young and I can hold you in my arms, a little boy again. You run to me and call my name. Nothing could part us then.

SHAKA

It has been a long time since I was young. I dreamed I had a mother once. Empty dreams. I have awakened from that sleep.

NANDI

You are indeed my son. Your heart has grown as cold as mine has been. I taught you well not to forgive. Do what you will. I am your mother still. Whatever life I lived, it was for you.

SHAKA

No, Mother. Let us have the truth before you die. You always served your own ends. Your only way to power—through me. And you did that very well.

NANDI

Whether well done or not I do not know. It all seems strange and long ago. And distant as a dream.
  (Weakly SHE reaches toward HIM.)
Take my hand now. Only that is real. All else is passed away.

> (SHAKA refuses to take her hand and turns away and starts toward the door. Her hand falls and her head falls to one side as SHE dies. SHAKA turns back to HER.)

SHAKA

Mother.
> (As HE realizes that she does not answer, he hurries to her side and kneels.)

Mother? Mother!

> (HE realizes that she is dead. He takes HER in his arms, HIS head bowed over her body. PAMPATA enters and kneels, followed by the SERVING WOMAN and the GUARD who kneel wailing.)

SHAKA

> (Arises and looks down at those who are kneeling.)

What grief is this? Do you call this mourning for your dead queen? You mourn like this!

> (In a frenzy, HE grabs the GUARD'S spear and cuts himself across the chest until the blood flows. He tears his garments and falls to his knees, throwing dust on his head. He cuts himself again.)

Draw blood, like this, and this! Let blood flow to show your grief.

> (HE rises and gestures menacingly to the GUARD.)

Kill all her servants, and send them beneath the earth to tell her that we mourn! She shall not go lonely on her way.

> (The frightened SERVING WOMAN backs away and flees from HIS presence. To the GUARD.)

Go, tell them the Queen is dead. Issue my orders. They will fast and mourn for her. No one will eat cattle or drink milk without my leave. No couple conceive a child to show their grief. I will show them how to mourn, like this and this. Kill all who show no grief! Every family will have a death to mourn. Go!

> (The GUARD exits.)

PAMPATA

> (Hesitating, fearfully reaching out to HIM.)

My lord—come away. I will mourn with you.

SHAKA

> (As if finally recognizing her, HE lowers the spear.)

Stay here. Prepare her body for the grave. No one must touch her without your leave. I will show them all how kings must mourn. With blood and death, I will show them all.

(HE exits in a frenzy. PAMPATA starts back appalled and turns to kneel by NANDI'S side. FRENZIED SOUND of DRUMS. BLACKOUT.)

END OF SCENE FIVE

ACT II: SCENE SIX

(PAMPATA'S hut. A campfire is at one side of the stage. PAMPATA is sitting on a stool by the fire with the firelight playing on her face. MBOPA enters and stands in the shadows beyond the firelight.)

PAMPATA
(Suddenly SHE looks up.)
Who is there? I see you in the shadows. Come forth. What do you want of me? Speak! Who are you?

MBOPA
One who seeks your help, Oh, House of Dreams.

PAMPATA
Come forth into the light and let me see your face.
(SHE stands. MBOPA comes forth out of the shadows and into the light from the fire.)
So the elders honor me. How can I serve you, Oh Counselor to the King?

MBOPA
By serving the people who need you now.

PAMPATA
What do they need?

MBOPA
Help only you can give. The Queen Mother has been dead these many moons. Our blood runs in torrents through this land. The Great Lion devours his own people. Our bones whiten the plain where the lions feed on men. The smell of death is everywhere.

PAMPATA
He mourns and gives you cause to mourn.

MBOPA

This kind of mourning is close to madness. The people groan under his heavy hand. No kraal is safe from his bloody claws. He has placed a corpse by every fire. He will destroy us all unless you intervene.

PAMPATA

I cannot turn his mind. He trusts no one now, not even me.

MBOPA

If he will listen to anyone, it is you. You must try to turn his course. The people can stand no more. There is open talk of rebellion. If there is a civil war, our enemies will take advantage of our strife and close in for the kill. The King will not order out his troops. Help us I beg of you. Plead our cause with him.

PAMPATA

And if he will not listen?

MBOPA

Then help us to rid the land of death.

PAMPATA

Be careful what you say. I am loyal to the king.

MBOPA

Then be loyal to the people first, if you are loyal to the king. He was one of us, before he was a king. If he seeks death, do not let the people die.

PAMPATA

You must not say these things to me.

MBOPA

I am old. Death holds no fear for me. I have lived my life that the Zulu might live in the traditions of our tribe. Let the ancestors be called to witness; I am content with that. I plead with you in their name and in the people's name.

PAMPATA
What would you have me do?

MBOPA
Speak to him in the people's name. Free the land of death. Beg him to lead us once again against our enemies. He was a great chief once. The people would remember that and follow if he chose to lead.

PAMPATA
And if he does not choose?

MBOPA
Then you must let the memory of his greatness live. All men must die. Only legends live beyond an earthly span.

PAMPATA
I will never betray him.

MBOPA
I do not ask that you betray him. Only do not stand between him and his fate. Listen to your voices in the night. Let the ancestors show the way. He will choose his path, and we but follow where he leads.

PAMPATA
I will find a way to speak to him in the people's name. So much I will promise, but nothing more.

MBOPA
We see into your heart. It is enough.

PAMPATA
It is unthinkable that he should not be king. As if the mountains were asked to fall.

MBOPA
Even mountains must wear away with time. Nothing stands forever.

PAMPATA

Who would rule in his place?

MBOPA

His brother, Dingane.

PAMPATA

Dingane cannot be trusted.

MBOPA

But we must begin with trust. Where else can we begin? Dingane is not a fool.

PAMPATA

Do you think we would be safe with him? We would be the first to die.

MBOPA

So be it, if the people live.

PAMPATA

What you have said will be safe with me.

MBOPA

I knew it. I did not have to ask.

PAMPATA

I will send you word. Go safely, Old Father.

MBOPA

And you, stay well, my child.

(HE exits. LIGHTS DIM. CAMPFIRE goes OUT. DRUMS RISE.)

END OF SCENE SIX

ACT II: SCENE SEVEN

(PAMPATA crosses the stage to meet MGOBOZI as HE enters from opposite side of the stage.)

MGOBOZI

You sent for me?

PAMPATA

Old friend, help me. I have tried to seek audience with the king, but he will not see me.

MGOBOZI

He takes counsel only with himself. He has given orders that no one come near him. I've sent messengers but been refused.

PAMPATA

How long has he been like this?

MGOBOZI

Since news came from the North. All day he broods alone, waiting for further news. But he will not act.

PAMPATA

What word has come?

MGOBOZI

Zwide's son has attacked to the north. Our outposts are hard pressed on every side. The time is growing critical, but no word from the king.

PAMPATA

He must be made to change his mind, or else he is destroyed and all the people with him. You must go to him. This may be his last chance to lead.

MGOBOZI

He will no longer listen to my advice, I tell you! I've tried.

PAMPATA

You must find a way to make him listen. Call up the courage of his youth when you two stood together against the enemy. Nothing could defeat you then. Stand with him once more, old friend. He must not die like this.

MGOBOZI

I'll try again and send you word. Go you well, Pampata.

PAMPATA

And you, old friend, stay well.

(THEY exit at opposite sides of the stage.)

END OF SCENE SEVEN

ACT II: SCENE EIGHT

(The Royal Kraal. TWO GUARDS stand apart holding spears and shields. As MGOBOZI enters, GUARDS block his path.)

MGOBOZI

I seek an audience with the king.

FIRST GUARD

He has given orders that no one pass.

MGOBOZI

Get out of my way! I have no time for words!
  (The GUARDS block his path and raise their spears. They are on the point of clashing with MGOBOZI.)
I must see the king!

SHAKA

(Enters from his royal hut.)
Must see the king? Does seeing make a king? If I put out your eyes, what am I then?

MGOBOZI

I have no time for riddles. Tell your guards to let me pass.

SHAKA

There's a riddle? Let you pass? Who are you?

MGOBOZI

Your oldest friend who stood with you at Qokli Hill and saved your life.

SHAKA

Friend? You call that "friend" who saved my life? I have lived to regret that many times.

MGOBOZI

The time for regret is over.

SHAKA
(HE gestures, and the GUARDS step back.)
Still brave, old "friend"? Haven't they told you that I am mad?

MGOBOZI

So are we all. I believe what I see.

SHAKA

Then you, too, are mad to believe only what you see. So are we all mad who believe the world is what it shows.

MGOBOZI

I see that the enemy are at our very gates.

SHAKA

Let them come. I'll open the gates myself. I'll show them who is mad.

MGOBOZI

Where is the Lion I once knew?

SHAKA

I do not know where he has gone. He dreamed of madness and of death.

MGOBOZI

What else is new? That men must die? I've heard that tale before. Are you the only one who dreams?

SHAKA

I have put on the mask of madness and cannot take it off.

MGOBOZI

Where is the man you were behind the mask?

SHAKA
He played at being king. The game begins to pall.

MGOBOZI
And I have played at war. Then play the drama out.

SHAKA
This time we cannot win. I have seen your death in battle and my own a later time.

MGOBOZI
I have seen my own death in a dream. Have we not met him many times before 'til he becomes an old, familiar friend? Would you sit shivering before the fire, a toothless lion limping toward old age? Let us taste the joy of battle once again before we go.

SHAKA
Yes, there was joy in that when we were young. To know the foe you face and not fight shadows.

MGOBOZI
Do you remember our victory at Qokli Hill, our backs together against the foe? Nothing could defeat us then!

SHAKA
Yes, when we were young. But now, victory or defeat? They are both the same.

MGOBOZI
Then what is there to lose? Let it go. Come, old friend, give the word. We've lived by the spear, you and I. It is a fitting death. But they will know our names before we go.

SHAKA
You almost make me young again, but it is too late.

MGOBOZI
(Looking at HIM in contempt.)
You are right. It is too late! There is nothing behind your mask.

(HE starts to turn away.)

SHAKA
Wait! Bring up your warriors. Prepare for our last battle. They will remember our names this day. I recognize you now—behind your mask. Honor is your name.

MGOBOZI
And I recognize you, Lion Among Men. We will meet again when the battle is joined.

SHAKA
We will meet again.
(MGOBOZI exits. SHAKA speaks to the GUARDS.)
Call my captains! Bring my shield and spear! Prepare for war!

(WAR DRUMS SOUND. SHAKA and the GUARDS exit.)

END OF SCENE EIGHT

ACT II: SCENE NINE

(Shaka's Royal Kraal. The WARRIORS have left the Stage. LIGHTNING FLASHES in green and yellow. THUNDER ROLLS. PAMPATA enters from stage Left and MBOPA from stage Right. PAMPATA looks anxiously at the sky. THEY meet in the center of the stage.)

PAMPATA
What news Mbopa?

MBOPA
The King is safe and leads his victorious army home. The people have gone out to bring them in.

PAMPATA
What of his friends?

MBOPA
Mgobozi is dead. He died a hero's death.

PAMPATA
Mgobozi dead? And Mzilikazi?

MBOPA
Mzilikazi has turned traitor and deserted to the north and taken his regiments with him.

PAMPATA
Nobela spoke the truth. Now the king must stand alone with no friends by him. His enemies will take this for a sign. I feel danger in the air. A storm is coming.

MBOPA
He must not be unguarded in the crowd. His enemies are everywhere.

                          PAMPATA
Go! Warn him!

                  (SOUND of victory DRUMS.)

                         THE CROWD
               (Off.)
Bayete! Shaka Zulu! Bayete!

                           MBOPA
Too late. They're here. They're praising his name with shouts of victory.

                  (SHAKA enters from stage right followed by his
                  WARRIORS. A CROWD of people appear to be
                  held back just out of sight at stage right.)

                         THE CROWD
Bayete! Shaka Zulu! Bayete!

                          PAMPATA
                  (Trying to speak to SHAKA as a WARRIOR bars
                  her way.)
My lord, hear me!
                  (To the WARRIOR.)
Let me pass!

                          WARRIOR
                  (Stepping forward and gesturing toward SHAKA.)
         Where is the praise singer who will sing his name?
         His roar was as thunder across the plain.
         Lion among men was our lord this day.
         On the field of battle he seized his prey.
         Sharp is his tooth and sharp his claw.
         We fought by the Lion's mighty law.

                      (SOUND of DRUMS.)

THE CROWD
Bayete! Shaka Zulu! Bayete!

(SHAKA holds up his arms for silence.)

WARRIOR
Where is Mgobozi, hero of men?
He fought the enemy with the strength of ten.
Where is the praise signer to sing his name?
Who fell in battle among the slain.

(SOUND of DRUMS.)

THE CROWD
Bayete! Shaka Zulu! Bayete!

SHAKA
(Acting out the events HE describes.)

I will sing the praises of Mgobozi, my oldest friend, the bravest warrior I have ever known. He died a hero's death, alone, facing the enemy with his back against a wall of rock. They surrounded him and closed in for the kill. Again and again and yet again he drove them back. He fought like one gone mad. Bleeding from head to foot with bloody foam upon his lips, he yet fought on, laughing in the teeth of death. Like a pack of wild dogs, they circled him but could not bring him down. I could not fight my way to his side.

As if my life were charmed, no spear could touch me. Across the space that separated us, Mgobozi shouted words of praise and cheer: "U-Zulu! Bayete! King of Kings! Bayete!" Then the enemy charged, twenty spears against his one, and pulled him to the ground. His last words were, "Sigidi! Shaka Zulu! Sigidi!" When he fell, the tide turned. We swept past where he lay and killed them all. They died—we live to die another day.

MBOPA
We sing the praises of Mgobozi! His name will live in honor, oh king, as long as the Zulu live. In time to come, they will remember him and you, oh king, protector of your people and their land.

SHAKA

We have brought Mgobozi home to join his ancestors. Bury him in the hide of a royal bull as befits a king. In time to come, let them remember Mgobozi who learned to rule himself and chose the only kingdom worth the price. Even kings must die, but only honor lives when men are gone.

> (DINGANE steps forward from behind SHAKA.)

DINGANE

You have given the word, oh King. Even kings must die! I will be your Praise Singer, and my sword will sing your praises.

> (As SHAKA turns, DINGANE draws a short spear from beneath his cloak and stabs SHAKA.)

MHLANGANA

> (Attacking SHAKA from behind, stabbing him in the back.)

And mine!

> (DINGANE'S MEN turn on the CROWD at stage right and drive them from the stage.)

DINGANE

> (Speaking directly to SHAKA, who is still standing, clutching his wounds.)

We have killed tyranny! Tyranny is dead!

SHAKA

There is a storm coming will flood this land. You will be too weak to hold it back. You are not fit to rule!

DINGANE

Let tyranny die that peace may live!

> (HE stabs SHAKA, who falls dead.)

(The SOUND of THUNDER is heard. LIGHTNING FLASHES.)

PAMPATA

(Standing in DINGANE'S way as he turns from SHAKA'S body.)

You have taken up the spear and will never let it go. You and your brothers will turn and rend each other. Beware, Mhlangana: Dingane will never let you live.

(To DINGANE.)

Strike! Hurry! What is one death more to you? I must go with him in that endless night.

DINGANE

(Stabbing PAMPATA with the spear and then running off stage shouting.)

Kill all our enemies! Peace with a spear!

MHLANGANA

(Following DINGANE, circling SHAKA'S body, afraid of it still.)

Peace with a spear!

(HE exits. PAMPATA falls.)

PAMPATA

Sigidi! Shaka Zulu! Sigidi!

(SHE dies. LIGHTS SLOWLY DIM. Distant THUNDER is HEARD. SOUND of DRUMS. FADE to BLACK.)

END OF SCENE NINE

ACT II: SCENE TEN (EPILOGUE)

(SOUND of DRUMS. The LIGHT SLOWLY FADES on SCENE TEN.)

NARRATOR
(Enters. Stands between the bodies of SHAKA and PAMPATA.)

A storm is coming. It is in the air. I feel it. The wind is cold. Stir the last embers of the dying fire, like this.

(HE stirs the fire, and it FLARES UP.)

Let it flame up to make a little space of light here where we are, for around us is the jungle and the night. And we are only men and women, hemmed in by darkness and by dreams, who live a moment and are gone. I have seen many things, but where are they now? It is all a dream and I am tired and old.

(SOUND of DISTANT THUNDER and DRUMS.)

Go home to your beds before the coming storm. What more is there to say? The tale is ended.

(SOUND of THUNDER and DRUMS stops abruptly. The stage is suddenly PLUNGED into total DARKNESS.)

END OF SCENE TEN

END OF ACT TWO

END OF THE PLAY

Appendix

Shaka
Readings and Awards and Honors

Staged Readings and Readings
2002 Afro-American Cultural Center at Yale University as part of the International Festiva of Arts and Ideas, New Haven, Connecticut.
2002 Playwrights Collective New Play Series, Brookfield Theatre for the Arts, Connecticut.
2000 The Schoolhouse Theatre Playwrights Workshop, Croton Falls, New York (developmental readings.

Awards and Honors
2003 Finalist, The Lark Theatre Company Playwrights Week, 2003.
2002 Chosen for Playwrights Collective New Play Series, Brookfield Theatre for the Arts, Connecticut.
2001 Finalist/Honorable Mention, Writer's Digest National Writing Competition (out of 19,000 entries).

About the Authors

Jan Henson Dow has won more than 150 national playwriting competitions, awards, and honors, including an NBC New Voices Award. Her plays have received numerous productions, workshops, and staged readings around the country, and her full-length plays have been published by Samuel French and Popular Play Service.

As a Professor at Western Connecticut State University, Dow directed the Playwriting Workshops and co-produced Western's Festival of New Plays. She has been the recipient of a number of playwriting grants, as well as grants for the new play festivals. She also taught playwriting workshops at the Osher Life Long Learning Institute at the University of South Carolina and at workshops around the country. Her articles and poems have appeared in such publications as *The New York Times*, *The Dramatists Guild Quarterly*, *Kansas Quarterly*, and *Indiana Review*. She co-authored *Writing the Award Winning Play* with Shannon Michal Dow, and they have just completed their first novel, *The Darkest Lies*. Jan is a member of the Dramatists Guild.

Robert Schroeder has won a number of playwriting competitions, including an NBC New Voices Award. His plays have been staged nationally. He served on the staff of *The Dramatist Guild Quarterly* and the Dodd-Mead *Best Plays* reference annuals. His reviews and theatre commentaries also appeared in *The Nation*, *Commonweal*, *New York*, and other periodicals. His anthology, *The New Underground Theatre*, was published by Bantam Books, and he was among the contributors to *Playwrights, Lyricists, and Composers on Theatre*, a Dodd-Mead hardcover. He has been retained professionally as a play/musical "doctor" for a number of Off Broadway productions.

Phosphene Publishing Company publishes books and DVDs relating to literature, history, the paranormal, film, spirituality, and the martial arts.

For other great titles, visit
phosphenepublishing.com

www.ingramcontent.com/pod-product-compliance
Lightning Source LLC
Chambersburg PA
CBHW061439040426
42450CB00007B/1122

4 unidades

The Song of the Cobweb

The Song of the Cobweb is a collection of poems that transports the reader to lands that are mystical and magical, to where Rimbaud once walked and where the normal rules of physics do not apply.

Something is slightly different, something is just out of focus, just out of reach - but if we squint and if we stretch it may just aid us on this strange unfathomable journey we are on. A journey where those who truly comprehend the boundaries governing the path we tread know full well that we must invent the rules as we go along...

Not all are aware of this; some have an inkling but may not have the courage to unrestrictedly throw everything into the wind to see what scatters where...

Some poets have this inkling, and some poets have the confidence to allow their lives to be governed by this knowledge.

This poet feels it, knows it and follows its haphazardness to see where it takes him; this unfettered, unrestricted abandon to the swaying notions of the rhythms of the undefinable...
The song of the Cobweb will take you on this journey with him.

RE-12

ISBN 978-1-9998215-8-6

£9.85